THE AMERICAN INDIAN
IN
AMERICAN LITERATURE
A Study in Metaphor

Elizabeth I. Hanson

Studies in American Literature
Volume 2

The Edwin Mellen Press
Lewiston/Queenston
Lampeter

Library of Congress Cataloging-in-Publication Data
Hanson, Elizabeth I.
    The American Indian in American literature ; a study in metaphor /
Elizabeth I. Hanson.
        p. cm. -- (Studies in American literature ; v. 2)
        Bibliography: p.
        Includes index.
        ISBN 0-88946-098-1
        1. American literature--History and criticism. 2. Indians in literature.
3. Metaphor. I. Title. II. Series: Studies in American literature (Lewiston,
N.Y.) ; v. 2.
PS173.I6H36 1988
810'.9'3520397--dc19   88-13958
                                                                      CIP

This is volume 2 in the continuing series
Studies in American Literature
Volume 2 ISBN 0-88946-098-1
SAL Series ISBN 0-88946-166-X

For information contact: **The Edwin Mellen Press**
Box 450   Box 67
Lewiston, New York   Queenston, Ontario
USA 14092   CANADA L0S 1L0
                        Mellen House
                   Lampeter, Dyfed, Wales
                UNITED KINGDOM SA48 7DY

Printed in the United States of America

Dedicated to:
My parents and my brother, Luther

TABLE OF CONTENTS

INTRODUCTION

"The whole of nature is a metaphor
of the human mind" Emerson, Nature
(1936)

In this book I am concerned to discover the metaphorical Indian in American literature. This figure has been designed by master writers of American fiction from Herman Melville and Henry David Thoreau to Mark Twain and William Faulkner and, in our own time, by Native American literary artists such as N. Scott Momaday and Leslie Marmon Silko. For each of these creators of visionary Indians, the wildness of the American terrain and the meaning of the indigenous population make available an imaginative force of words. To comprehend that wild land and the wild men, or so they seemed, who first inhabited it, American writers search for an existence and significance within themselves.

The best studies of the American Indian in American literature are varied and complex in approach and critical imagination. D. H. Lawrence begins the scholarly evaluation of the Indian figure in Studies in Classic American Literature (1923); he envisages the hero of the American monomyth as "hard, isolate, stoic, and a killer," doomed, like the Indian, to extinction and using the "dark races" to help "in this ghastly maniacal hunt which is our doom and our suicide."[1] Leslie Fiedler recasts Lawrence's thesis in The Return of the Vanishing American(1968) by making the Indian one of his "basic myths" inherent to the American mind.

Richard Slotkin in his Regeneration Through Violence (1973) speculates on how American heroes in early popular American literature seek to acquire power over nature through acts of terror and violence. Roy Harvey Pearce explores the Indian in America through his history of the

2

idea of primitivism in <u>The Savages of North America</u> (1953, rev. ed. <u>Savagism and Civilization</u>, 1965). In the best and most useful examination of the Indian in America, Robert Berkhofer writes a history of the <u>White Man's Indian</u> (1978) of far-ranging scope of vision. Because of the depth and range of his history, Berkhofer limits his discussion of the white man's literary Indians to several pages of careful, if all too brief analysis.

A full-scale critical study of the nature of the Indian metaphor as it is formed by master writers of American fiction is needed. For American literary artists the Indian figure--a being quite distinct from the actual Native American population--proves a rich source of subtle and interpenetrating imagery which ranges from the fictional to the ideological and, at times, the anti-ideological. Thus, for Henry David Thoreau to write a poem is to "take a scalp," as he discovers in creative violence a richness that heartens and enlightens by its seemingly inexhaustible vitality. In <u>Moby-Dick</u> Herman Melville designs a Polynesian-Indian, Queequeg, who contains within the "living parchment" of his skin "a mystical treatise on the art of attaining truth" in an inscrutable civilized world. For William Faulkner, too, the Indian figure becomes a source of knowledge from another realm of experience; Sam Fathers teaches the young Ike McCaslin in <u>Go Down, Moses</u> and passes on his consciousness of the wild to "the white boy, marked forever, and the old man sired on both sides by savage kings, who had marked him . . . so that he could continue to live past the boy's seventy years and then eighty years, long after the man himself had entered the earth as chiefs and kings enter it." Here the vision of the Indian becomes inextricably shaped by the aesthetic concern for perpetuity, for objects and meanings that endure in a world of exterminations and endings. To dig to the roots of American Indian metaphors is to locate images commensurate with America's indigenous nature. To gather the spirits found there, American master writers use the role of the Indian figure as a kind of prophet-shaman who will assist them in their own attempts at radical transformation of the self and of their civilized society. What also emerges from the achievements of these creators of Indian metaphors is their effort to repossess the Indian and the spiritual and aesthetic experiences he represents before the Indian is utterly extinguished. Their art of the Indian, then, is not simply an end, but a springboard, one that elevates, at least the white man, to a vantage point from which he commands life, even the Indian's life. From such a perspective American master writers envision figures impervious to the destructive powers of civilized society's institutions and privy to all the secrets of the Indian's visionary imagination.

NOTES

1   D.H. Lawrence, <u>Studies In Classic American Literature</u> (New York, 1923), p. 160.

CHAPTER ONE:
SOURCES OF VISION

"We bind ourselves together by taking hold of each other's hands so firmly and forming a circle so strong that if a tree should fall upon it, it could not shake or break it, so that our people and grandchildren shall remain in the circle in security, peace and happiness." Dekaniwidah as told to Hiawatha.[1]

"Savages we call them because their Manners differ from ours, which we think the Perfection of Civility; they think the same of theirs." Benjamin Franklin[2]

American civilization as we know it begins with an essential disruption of the previous order of Europe. The emigration from Europe to America leads to instability, dissonance and disorder that threaten and ultimately undermine much of Indian tribal culture. Amid such ruinous circumstances one way of absorbing and transcending conflict is through the transformative power of the imagination.

Deserted by allies and defeated in war, with their hunting grounds lost forever and their cornfields devastated, the Seneca and the Iroquois face a generation of despair. Then, in 1799, through the vision of one of the Indians' leaders, they make a kind of peace between their threatened Indian culture and the white American one. At the point of death from alcoholism and already being prepared for burial, Handsome Lake in a hallucinatory state has a vision in which the Good Spirit reveals to him a new way of life. Fearing death from sickness or from witchcraft, Handsome Lake has drunkenly sung the Ohgiwe, the sacred song of the Chanters of the Dead; and when he sobers, he feels guilty for his sin, which only adds to his distress. A broken man, Handsome Lake, has a first vision in which three angels came from heaven to explain that his illness comes from a drunken way of life--all the Indians drink too much, and this is the cause of their present state. The angels then conduct him on a journey through heaven and hell and explain that the Good Spirit has ordered that he was to instruct the Indians in a new manner of life. After a miraculous recovery, Handsome Lake then propagates an austere code of beliefs which not only warns the Seneca away from alcohol, witchcraft, and wife-beating, but also counsels literacy in English and the practice of agriculture. Conscious of the self-destructiveness of the Indian warrior values in a dominant white world, Handsome Lake is able to turn his men into farmers and rechannel the hunter values of physical courage and prowess into more adaptive cultural patterns: many of his descendents became the "high steel" workers on American bridges and skyscrapers.

Interpenetrated within the new code were apocalyptic and millenial expectations resembling the Christian promises of heaven and hell, but in this system heaven is reserved for good Senecas; no whites are to be admitted. The world is to be destroyed in flames, and the wicked whites are to go to hell, where they will suffer in the manner recalling the old Iroquois torture of war prisoners. Even George Washington, the best of the whites, hangs in limbo between heaven and hell.[3]

The doctrine of Handsome Lake is a "mixture of the old and new, in part harking back to the good old days of the past, in part a practical and drastic accommodation to new times--from being a frontier slum folk, the Iroquois become the best adapted and most populous Indian group in the East."[4] The appearance of a messianic figure who touches off a new wave of morality, codifies a new approach to life, and thus revitalizes the society in its time of trouble should sound a familiar note not only to whites who have their own mythologies, but to the Seneca and Iroquois as well. About 1450 the Indian, Hiawatha, is said to have had a vision in which a supernatural creature named Dekanawidah appeared before him and "dictated a code for the revitalization of Iroquois society" which Hiawatha carried from village to village, recruiting disciples who regarded him as a prophet.[5] Hiawatha's visions served to strengthen the many distant, often desperate Indian villages, bind them together, and like Handsome Lake's preachings, make Iroquois less vulnerable to attack from without and to division from within. [6]

Such a search for wholeness seems rarely to succeed without the intervention of imaginative symbols of perception through metaphor. What remains constant in these and all visionary experience is the return to origins, the awakening of primal and powerful emotions free of past limitations, and the reempowering of a renewed self. The new rites and rules serve to make a kind of peace between the conflicting orders of the new world and the old one. The healing that is accomplished is curative in and of itself. In a fundamental way it ceases to matter that the world never ended, or the buffalo never returned. What does matter was the rite and the vision which allow the individual to come into contact with emotions "whose hurtfulness, both psychic and somatic, came chiefly of being denied, that permitted a transcendence of the 'split' state by putting individuals back into touch with the deeper levels of their own being and with each other."[7]

The parallels between the vision of Handsome Lake and the creators of Indian metaphors in American literature are stimulating: each locate in the symbols of imaginative revitalization a vision of society organized around concepts of reciprocity, spirituality, and community. With the passage of time, and with the steady growth of the white population, it becomes apparent to some individuals that one group of people in North America who are upholding these values, and organizing their society around them, are the Indians who are being driven from the very land they first possessed.

This paradox became all the more poignant when we remember that from Roger Williams to William Penn to Thomas Jefferson the notion of transplanted Europeans building a virtuous society in cities on the hill courses through the writings and emotions of the American immigrants. It is true that many colonists come venturing across the Atlantic only for material gain, but many others see the wilderness of North America as a place where tired, corrupt, materialistic, self-seeking Europeans might begin a new life.[8]

Melville and Thoreau and, later, Faulkner stand in awe of the Indian traits of generosity, bravery, spirituality, and community. These American artists present Indians who embody the virtues of Christianity almost without effort in a region where white Americans, while attempting to build their society with similar values, are actually creating a world of individualism, or mercantilism, and of a country which uses its wilderness and abuses its black population. Possessing the kind of innocence, as Gary Nash observes, that beckoned destruction,[9] the Indians in Thoreau and Melville and Faulkner's Indian metaphors, not only often refuse to reproach or expose the whites, but even make over to the whites their tribal fortune, the American wilderness. The Indians, as envisioned by these white American artists, hold out the possibility that the dehumanizing cycle of destruction may be remade. The basic intention of their art is to transform and thus defuse the potential threat by the process of art. Through a strategy of image making they attempt to make the Indian's presence defined on "white" terms.

Through a process of delienating, they seek to lessen the potential danger of the unknown "other." As Tony Tanner has observed in the context of another form of disruption, adultery, "as the sense of the inadequacy and provisionality of the normative and prescriptive categories governing behavior increased, so did the temple of the great bougeois novel begin to dismantle itself and turn into something else."[10] In American literature the novel turns toward the alien, the amazing, at times, the violent Indian, perhaps as a means of displacing and projecting, and thereby releasing white Americans' own sense of alienation onto this "other." To tame and domesticate the ambivalently perceived Indian reflects the need to "civilize" or control disruptive power. Also evident is the wish that the seemingly now controlled Indian may be transformed back to being an alien presence in order to release and free not merely himself but those around him who also feel thwarted. This complex of motives provides "one of the permanently generative themes of Western literature."[11] The paradoxical presence of alienation offers a constant threat to the society as a whole and an attack on the culture itself, revealing it be arbitrary and absolute. In such a freed and freeing terrain of the mind the Indian metaphor is discovered and made potent.

James Fenimore Cooper's Leather Stocking:
Metaphor of the Middle Ground.

The imagination of the Indian in American literature is one of the three great historical resources of the American fiction writer as William Howard Gardiner defined them: the Colonial period, the Revolution, and the Indian Wars.[12] The question of how to make an American literature preoccupies American writers from Royall Tyler to Henry James to Robert Frost. The necessity for discovering native materials is insistently affirmed. Thus, Charles Brockden Brown in the preface to Edgar Huntly (1799) remarks that "the sources of amusement to the fancy and instruction to the heart that are peculiar to ourselves are . . . numerous and inexhaustible."[13] James Fenimore Cooper in his Notions of the Americans observes that after the lack of international copyright, "the second obstacle against which American literature has to contend is in the poverty of materials.[14] Later Hawthorne, writing in response to Cooper's epic treatment of Indian materials, writes "no writer can be more secure of a permanent place in our literature than the biographer of Indian chiefs." When Hawthorne speaks as Grandfather, one of the characters in a children's story, he describes himself as "shut out from the most peculiar field of American fiction I do abhor an Indian story."[15]

While the writings of Washington Irving may be seen to bring American writing into English literature, James Fenimore Cooper is the first successful author to bring America itself into its literature. In so doing Cooper establishes the theme of the Indian with which major authors including Melville, Thoreau, Twain, and Faulkner would deal. Cooper provides them with what he did not possess: a characterization of what the Indian in fiction could represent.

The Indian, as Cooper knew him, could, in the 1820's, "be chiefly sought west of the Mississippi, to be found in any of his savage grandeur.[16] The frontier had been pushed across the Missouri, and the

Indians, at this point quite powerless, ceased to present a threat to the advance of civilization in the East. Cooper's daughter, Susan Fenimore Cooper, outlined an extensive course of readings on "Indian life and character," which she believed the author undertook in preparation for the writing of his first Indian novel, The Last of the Mohicans (1826). In an effort to come to know the increasingly distant way of Indian life, Miss Cooper recounts that her father examined the "earlier writers on those subjects, Heckwelder (sic), Charlevoix, Penn, Smith, Elliot (sic), Colden, . . . the narratives of Lang (sic), of Lewis and Clarke, of Mackenzie."[17] Further, she suggests that Cooper made a variety of contacts with Indian delegations and visits to Washington "for the purpose of closer observation, and with a view also to gathering information from the officers and interpreters who accompanied them."[18] Cooper's intimate knowledge of the primitive life of the Indian is gained almost wholly from missionaries and explorers. He is, as Robert E. Spiller observed, "too late for first-hand observation of his Indians in anything resembling their native state; but he was likewise too early for accurate historical and scientific knowledge of their racial characteristics and backgrounds."[19]

It is within Natty Bumppo that Cooper creates not an historical or scientific means of knowledge, but a metaphor of the middle ground, a model to examine through visionary consciousness the relation between the democratic American and the native inhabitants of America.[20] Such a new theme, new to the novel in English, required a new form. Natty inhabits a middle ground between civilized men and the wild. His democratic integrity, which makes him the moral equal of the very best civilized men, is derived from nature and from the Indian.[21] The fact that Natty is a white Christian who possesses a fear of Indian paganism as well as an admiration of Indian life makes of his experience a microcosm for the uneasy ambivalence of relations between Indians and whites.

It is the terrain between, the territory out of ultimate control, the area out of civilized bounds, which so stimulates the imagination, and which comes, for Thoreau and Melville, to represent that very imagination. Yet for

Cooper, who is inventing that mental space in fiction, it is the fact and treatment of his pathfinder, the man who literally makes and takes that space between civilization and the wild, that is most stimulating and most definitively American.

Too white to be an Indian and too wild to be truly civilized, Natty is a symbol for this fundamental contradiction. In The Prairie (1827) Cooper represents an anatomy of the course of American civilization with Natty assuming a central role and value. As civilization moves forward across the prairie, Natty moves ahead, slightly beyond it, and in so doing reflects the physical, if not the moral direction, it will follow:

> The march of civilization with us, has a strong analogy to that of all coming events, which are known "to cast shadows before." The gradations of society, from the state which is called refined to that which approaches barbarity as connection with an intelligent people will readily allow, are to be traced from the bosom of the States, where wealth, luxury and the arts are beginning to seat themselves, to those distant and ever-receding borders which mark the skirts and announce the approach of the nation, as moving mists precede the signs of the day.[22]

Here Cooper establishes two extreme possibilities, the "refined" and "barbarity." Natty occupies the middle ground between the contrasting culture Cooper defines in his own version of evolutionary anthropology. Within the cultural isolation that Natty chooses quite deliberately, Cooper designs a form from which to examine the idea of the geographical isolation of America itself--a separate continent and a wild landscape. Natty is conscious of the essential contradictions inherent to this idea of America, for the idea of primitive gifts of a wild nature and the ideal of endless progress of civilization come in direct confrontation, precisely because of the richness of the American landscape. It is the "swarms of the restless people which are ever found on the skirts of American society" in order "to plunge into these endless and unexplored regions"[23] who seek wealth and security by taming the west for their own use.

How to reconcile the necessity for and the difficulty of taming what has been "savage" is the essential imaginative problem of the Leather Stocking Saga. Ellen Wade inquires of the pathfinder in The Prairie: "tell me, do you then actually live alone in this desert district, old man; is there really none here beside yourself?" And he responds, "There are hundreds, nay, thousands of the rightful owners of the country, roving about the plains; but few of our own color."[24] The process by which the white characters in the Saga gradually Europeanize the American landscape leads inevitably to violence and corruption on both sides. But as the trapper explains to Mahtoree, the "wily Teton" chief, "The Master of Life looks with an open eye on his children who die in a battle that is fought for the right; but he is blind and his ears are shut to the cries of an Indian who is killed while plundering or doing evil to his neighbor."[25] That Cooper's intention here is irony is not clear; he points out that the mercy of God extends to "his children who die in a battle that is fought for the right," but then observes that the "Indian" who plunders or does evil is ignored by God. No mention is made of white plunder or civilized evil.

To seek reconciliation between the two opposing claims not merely for the American landscape but also for moral justification is to engage in a complex imagination quest. Here Cooper's metaphor of the pathfinder of the middle ground is crucial. Only Natty, who moves from one culture to the other, and who deliberately isolates himself from both, can discover the terms of a transcendent reality which Europeanizes the Indians and Indianizes the whites. In such a vision, the corruptions of Indian or white society are essentially ignored as having little ultimate significance "Natur' is much the same, let it be covered by what skin it may . . .what the experience of a long life tells me," Natty observes, "is the common cravings of man."[26] In such a version of "experience," all wrongdoing is bowdlerized into virtual meaninglessness because all men do wrong. Corruption is part of the "common" nature of humanity, simply a kind of

14

"craving" for what men do not possess. In Cooper's creation of a middle ground evil itself is reduced to a common and inevitable natural greed. Natty, "unlike most of those who lived a border life," between Indians and whites, is described by Middleton as uniting the "better instead of the worst qualities of the two people."[27]   Cooper's Leatherstocking becomes a metaphoric being fleeing the corruptions of Society yet limited by his own escape. In courage he was the equal of his red associates; in warlike skill, being better instructed, their superior. In short, he was a noble shoot from the stock of human nature, which never could obtain its proper elevation and importance, for no other reason, than because it grew in the forest."[28] His virtues of simplicity, of uncontrived "sterling" worth, of adventure and exploit, make the pathfinder a mythic figure to be valued by both Indians and whites, a being who mediates between their seemingly inherent prejudices against one another.

Leatherstocking seeks to overcome the racial prejudice and civilized over-refinements of Middleton and the other whites in The Prairie. For example, when Middleton impatiently demands of pathfinder whether the party is to be taken by the Sioux: "Is it an Indian you see?" Leatherstocking replies, "Redskin or Whiteskin, it is much the same friendship and use can tie men as strongly together in the woods as in the towns--aye, and for that matter stronger."[29]   Here Cooper establishes a moral vision of the potential relation between Indians and whites through kinship. Between young warriors such as the scout and Uncas, Cooper explores the relations between Indians and whites that will evolve into a new imaginative American form. The journey of white and dark companions through the American forest into the deeper regions of the self is Cooper's metaphorical contribution. His invention, the pathfinder, demands, "What the world of America is coming to, and where the machinations and inventions of its people are to have an end, the Lord, he only knows."[30] Leatherstocking acts as both a transitional and transcending force in a world with an unknowable and potentially disturbing end.   Always reassuring to white serving the whites, yet sympathetic to and able to cope with the Indians, pathfinder serves an essential need for mediation.

Through such a symbol anxiety is assuaged, ambiguity mitigated. Though pathfinder can note "now much has the beauty of the wilderness been deformed,"[31] he does nothing ultimately to prevent such deformation. In fact the very destruction of the wilderness occurs along the paths he finds and others follow. Even what he perceives as the crucial worth of the best of the Indians for white Americans is lost: "Poor reason, I allow; but still there is a great deal of the man in the Indian. Ah's me! Your Delaware were the red-skins of which America might boast; but few and scattered is that mighty people, now."[32] The last of the most valuable Indians, at least those most valuable to the whites, vanish. Like his treasured favorite path, his treasured favorite Indians are destroyed by the force of those who would use them.

At the end of all his efforts Leatherstocking stands, even in death, in the middle, supported by Middleton, the white man, on the one side and by Hardheart, the Indian, on the other as each "involuntarily extended a hand to support the form of the old man."[33] Middleton, whose name connotes his center of being in the middle of civilized forms and civil government, here upholds one version of experience while Hardheart sustains the other in a meeting of consciousness in the American landscape. Natty's character within the Saga evolves gradually from one of a number of minor figures "reflecting the range of American[34] society" to becoming an experiment in form, a metaphor of a journey between two worlds. The representative stature of Leatherstocking is ambiguous. As Sacvan Bercovitch has observed, he is "the creation of Cooper's readers--a reflection of their response to the frontier."[35] But Natty is also an imaginative creation that grows out of Cooper's own gradually accruing sense of pathfinder's significance as transcending and mediating symbol. He represents not only continuity but interpenetration between writer and reader, for Natty develops partly in response to Cooper's sense of his audience and also in terms of individual experience in American society. If a simpler cruder metaphor of mediation and of voyage into American experience than the spiritual and aesthetic quests of Thoreau and Melville and Faulkner, Cooper's imagination of such a metaphor is, indeed, an influential beginning. For example, Melville writes, "his works are among the earliest I can remember, as in my boyhood producing a vivid and awakening power upon my mind."[36] Cooper creates a metaphorical mediating frontiersman to explain and reveal a vanishing physical wilderness. For Thoreau, Melville, and Faulkner the aesthetic impulse is both more difficult and more challenging; they create a spiritual frontier, whether at Walden Pond, on the Pequod, or in the Big Woods, in visionary consciousness that recaptures by means of metaphor the presence of the Indian:

> The white man comes, pale as the dawn with a load of thought, with a slumbering intelligence as a fire raked up, knowing well what he knows... He buys the Indian's moccasins and baskets, then buys their hunting grounds, and at length forgets where he is buried and ploughs up his bones.[37]

Henry Wadsworth Longfellow:

Designing an American Myth of the Indian

Henry Wadsworth Longfellow defines his own American myth of Indian-white relations in <u>Hiawatha</u> (1855). While borrowing from Henry Rowe Schoolcraft's collections of Indian tales and legends--<u>Algic Researches, History of the Indian Tribes</u>, and <u>Oneonta</u>--Longfellow deploys his own range of aesthetic strategies. He romanticizes actual Indian experience, he emphasizes tribal violence, he idealizes white exploration of America, he defines Hiawatha in cosmic, heroic terms, and he seeks to forge a socially reassuring vision of America for his white audience. Always Longfellow is exploring a trail of inner images of Indian death and extinction. Through a series of such images Longfellow works to suggest implicit and comforting constraints of form, and revealing and expiating kinds of order within his <u>Hiawatha</u> cosmology.

In the seemingly limitless space and absence of civilized form of the American landscape, Longfellow searches the experience of the American Indian as it is filtered through the research of Indian observers and recorded for and by white men. The American terrain's distinctive characteristic was its wildness. The American poet's distinctive characteristic might be to praise and preserve that wildness within white men's metaphors. Ultimately, Longfellow seeks to restrain and retrain those artifacts and vestiges of American Indian culture which reach him into an American mythological formulation ordered and controlled in terms acceptable, indeed pleasing, to his white audience. He controls the "wildness" of the Indian by placing it within the social context of the white man.

Longfellow's process of mythologizing the American Indian is first recorded in a notebook entitled, "Sketches of New England," which he kept while studying languages in France, Spain, Italy, and Germany prior to assuming the professorship of modern Languages at Bowdoin College. In

Dresden surrounded by the riches of European culture, Longfellow explores American Indian materials and white history of emigration to the new world, and in the process he determines the outlines of Evangeline, Hiawatha, and The Courtship of Miles Standish in the late eighteen-twenties. For example, he suggests to himself sketches on "The Pilgrim Fathers and the Aborigines of the Land--their characters and circumstances contrasted," one on "Down East. The Missionary of Arcadie," one on "The Grey-eyed man. An Indian of the Wyandot Tribe," and one on the "Tale of the Ebbing wave.--Tale of the White Cloud."[38] By the eighteen thirties Longfellow had first established himself at Bowdoin, from 1829 to 1835, and then moved on to assume a professorship at Harvard College. During the same period Henry Rowe Schoolcraft published some of the first of what would become a large and influential body of materials relating to the American Indian. In a much read essay in an issue of the North American Review dated July, 1837, Schoolcraft published "History and Languages of the North American Indians." (In the same issue Longfellow published a review of Nathaniel Hawthorne's Twice-Told Tales). In Schoolcraft's article he wrote of exactly the potential for literature Longfellow had pondered in his sketch notebook in Dresden several years before. Schoolcraft observed: "The early history of the aborigines is taking a deep hold on literary attention in America. Materials for its illustration have, from time, appeared, rather, however, as the result of casual, than of professed research."[39] Schoolcraft's signal to his contemporary American literary artists was not lost on Longfellow.

By the mid-forties Longfellow and Thoreau also, who at this time began his Indian Books by comparing Schoolcraft's and other Indian scholars' choice of Indian subjects with his own interests--began to mine the Indian vein. While Thoreau constantly sought to make of the Indian a being out of his own mind, Longfellow chose a different Indian, one largely devised from Schoolcraft's legends and one which reflected a cultivated and regulated use of "professed research" eminently suitable for the scholarly Longfellow's mode of poetic operation vis-à-vis his American audience.

In the writing of <u>Evangeline</u> in the mid-forties Longfellow turned to Schoolcraft for illustrative legends, and then Longfellow began his long perusal of the by this time considerable number of volumes of ethnographic materials Schoolcraft had amassed. On 22 June 1854 Longfellow wrote, "I have at length hit upon a plan for a poem on the Indians, which seems to me the right one, and the only. It is to weave together their beautiful traditions into a whole."[40] This "plan" for the writing of <u>Hiawatha</u> required that Longfellow order the legends of Schoolcraft into a tapestry of unity and coherence of Longfellow's own making. His focus is not the Indians' experience, but the shape and wholeness of uniting poetic process.

His process is a mythologizing one, and his purpose is to influence a wide audience of white Americans on their own American epic-making responsibilities in the "new world." Longfellow does not employ the Indian as a metaphor of spiritual and aesthetic retreat from civilization into a higher realm of inner meaning. Instead Longfellow sees in the Indian and his legends a prefiguring of the white man's obligation to serve civilization and his own white society. Longfellow's Indians are not examples of pure escapism or silly indulgences; they are elements in Longfellow's epic recreation of American history.

The essence of Longfellow's Indian vision then is not the Indian but the white man's responsibility to construct a successful civilization on what was the Indians' terrain no longer. In <u>Evangeline</u> the Indians are portrayed as "Ishmael's children, staining the desert with their blood," and the responsibility for a blood-stained North American continent is given to the "savage" natives who maraud and destroy white men. (Part II, Canto IV, 18-23). Longfellow uses Schoolcraft's Indian sources in <u>Evangeline</u>--one about "Mowis, the bridegroom of snow" from Schoolcraft's <u>Oneonta, or Characteristics of the Red Race</u> (1845) and one concerning the "fair Lilinau" and her phantom from <u>Algic Researches</u>: <u>Comprising Inquiries Respecting the Mental Characteristics of the North American Indians</u>

(l839)--but Longfellow stresses how the white man's civilizing role transforms North America. More than simply patriotism or literary nationalism, Longfellow seeks in Schoolcraft's Indian gatherings lessons for the white man who must deal with "savages" while assuming responsibility for the creation of Idealized American "civilization" in this new terrain.

Hiawatha is designed to provide a much larger frame for revealing this essential lesson than Miles Standish or Evangeline, and in Hiawatha Longfellow shifts the angle of vision from the colonists to the pre-history of their experience. Hiawatha is an epic retelling of the origins of Indian-white relations in America. Its white readers are introduced to Indian legends and able to enjoy nature imagery, but Longfellow's tales and his recreation of a world where man enjoys communion with nature is designed to yield a perspective for viewing American civilizing forces in the Indians' land.

The natural world of the Indian is of pure enjoyment in poetry. The "stories", the Indian "legends and traditions" derive "from the forests and the prairies" and even the voice of the poet is conceived as a "wild fowl" (Introduction, 1-35). The image of wild fowl indigenous to the American continent, singing the "wild and wayward" poetry, leads quickly to death, to the "neglected graveyards" of the nearly extinguished native population. Even at the end of the Introduction to the poem Longfellow has shifted already from his natural setting to an imaginary political history; in the process he seeks to convince his reader "that in even savage bosoms there are longings, yearning, strivings for the good they comprehend not" (Intro. 87-115). But Longfellow comprehends those "strivings," at least those of the white man, and he uses them to provide a platform for viewing the conflicts that have swept across the American continent and through American history as it is created by white men and white poets, also.

In Canto I Longfellow begins immediately to reveal the savagery of the Indians' experience prior to the coming of the white men, by implication. The nature of the Indians' seeming blessed innocence and peace turns demonic in <u>The Peace Pipe</u> canto as the Indians are portrayed as people of "quarrels," of "war and blood-shed," of "vengeance," and of "wranglings and dissensions" (Canto I, 108-111). Gitche Manito, the "Master of Life," offers to send a "Prophet"--Hiawatha, son of Wenonah and the West-Wind--who would guide and teach the nations of the peace they could not create themselves. At the same time Gitche Manito warns the gathered Indian nations who hold in "their hearts the feuds of ages" that if they do <u>not</u> listen to the counsel of Hiawatha they will "fade away and perish" at the hands of other forces. Manito, the Great Spirit, smiles at "his helpless children" as they bury their hatchets, but amid this false peace there lurks violence still. For "dark below them flowed the water, soiled and stained with streaks of crimson, as if blood were mingled with it" (Canto I, 116-164).

There is a chaos and potential for violence in the Indians' natural world that emerges from Longfellow's vision of Indian-White history. The poet limits the violent implications in <u>The Peace Pipe</u> canto by offering a countervalent possibility through Hiawatha's teachings--the Indians are provided with a Christ-like figure and the means of salvation--but that very potential is undercut. In the images of only silent acquiescence and bloody, dark streams of violence within, the Indians are portrayed as having little chance to overcome their essential "thirst for violence." The smoking peace pipes mask inner apprehensions and underlying tensions within the Indians. A Hiawatha might guide and counsel, a Gitche Manito might warn and control, but only at the hands of the white men would the violence cease. And the cost of genuine Indian peace would be death.

<u>The Peace-Pipe</u> and <u>The Four Winds</u> (Canto I & Canto II) each illustrate the peril of Indian violence. That hostility is meant to offend the white reader's search for civilized order and to legitimatize white violence toward the Indian as a necessary evil designed to prevent further destruction. Hiawatha emerges from this threatening vision of Indian ferocity--he himself is the offspring of a rape--and as a being of complex and mediating sources of vision. His mythic character is defined through

his god-like nature and half-noble birth, and the progress of his life is designed to reflect a traditional hero's struggle for visionary consciousness. Yet Hiawatha's epic quest is framed to reveal a precise angle of vision, that of the white men's view of Indian violence as irremediable except through extermination.

Hiawatha himself is portrayed as subtly violent. In Longfellow's vision, all Indians, even the god-like Hiawatha, are capable of guile and vengeance, so it is not surprising that in Canto IV Hiawatha meets his father, Mudjekeewis, the West Wind, and seeks to avenge his mother's honor by deadly conflict. Although Hiawatha fails to kill his father--the immortal cannot be killed--Hiawatha receives a prize of valor; he is assigned the role of living among his people in order to cleanse the earth from all that harms it (Canto IV, 219-235). Through fasting and mortal combat, through the guidance of Chibiabos, the musician, and the strong man, Kwasind, Hiawatha assumes his redemptive battles with the evil forces of his world. Hiawatha's excursions through the Indians' visionary universe recapitulate the cycle of violence articulated earlier in the introduction to the poem as well as reflect traditional trials of the epic hero. Canto X, "Hiawatha's Wooing," and Canto XI, "Hiawatha's Wedding Feast," interrupt the tale of Hiawatha's violent progress with a counterpoint love theme. Temporarily, Hiawatha has performed his epic task; his world had "buried the bloody hatchet, buried was the dreadful war-club, buried were all warlike weapons, and the war-cry was forgotten" (Canto XIII, 7-10). But despite the sacred rituals and magic circles Hiawatha and Minnehaha enact, they are threatened by ferocious ravens and Hiawatha quickly destroys them. The cycle of violence reemerges, as Hiawatha's vengeance again becomes the principal narrative concern of the poem.

Death and violence are portrayed as the tribal experience. Everywhere Hiawatha discovers "how all things fade and perish" (Canto XIV, 2). In response to his vision of a dying past of "dreams and visions" Hiawatha invents "Picture Writing" as a means of recording some small element of the Indian past for those who might discover it. The implications of Hiawatha's Picture Writing are particularly revealing, for Hiawatha notes that without a written language the experience of the Indians is a "secret message." Even if the bearer of the message "learns our secret," he may pervert it, may betray it, may reveal it unto others" (Canto XIV, 27-34). That the Indians possessed no fully formed written records of their traditions, that they were forced to rely on the white men's languages and on white men's records of their legends, such as Schoolcraft's or Longfellow's, is the unspoken irony of the Canto.

Despite all his efforts to restrain evil in the Indian world, Hiawatha remains a target of violence. The evil spirits seek to molest and destroy him and all he loves, and Hiawatha responds now not with violence but with depression and "lamentation." The death of Chibiabos, Hiawatha's brother, imposes the reality of personal loss on the hero of the poem, but Hiawatha loses his capacity to act as he has always done in other moments of crisis throughout the poem. Although the Medicine men come to console him and although Hiawatha himself recovers and goes on to share the sacred arts of healing to mortal men, the essential shape of Hiawatha's characterization as heroic questor changes in Canto XV "Hiawatha's Lamentation" Longfellow has designed an Indian hero as violent and then redirects that design to show the Indian hero as victim. Death of Indians in theme and imagery is the focus of the poem, but Longfellow is committed to the crucial strategy of explaining as well as articulating that death. Hiawatha as violent victim fulfills Longfellow's strategic vision perfectly.

Violence and victimization are cyclical; violent behavior begets victims and victims respond with violence, when they are able, toward those who have victimized them. For example, in Canto XVI the jealous Pau-Puk-Keewis, having grown "tired of Hiawatha's wisdom," tries to taunt and damage Hiawatha (Canto XVI, 69). Although Hiawatha and his hunters try to kill Pau-Puk-Keewis, their victim's soul still survives to taunt them and they are forced to exert ever more power to control it. Ultimately, Hiawatha ends the wild adventures of Pau-Puk-Keewis and transforms this

representative figure from a human being into a trancendent image in the
heavens. The wildness of the human Indian, in Longfellow's vision here, is
replaced by a reassuring and safe figure removed from human experience
through extermination.

All the remaining cantos of the poem continue to devolve out of
images of death. In microcosm, Longfellow explores the meaning of the
extinction of the Indians by the white men through the cosmic drama of
Hiawatha's own experience with death. He expresses violence and hatred,
he himself is victimized, he experiences personal loss through the death of
his family members, he is depressed and saddened, he seeks to heal and
console Indian survivors of death, he searches for transcendent and
transformative possibilities of life after death, and he imagines a visionary
portrayal of death among the Indians just prior to his own mortal end.
Thus, immediately following the transformed death of Pau-Puk-Keewis is
the story of "The Death of Kwasind" in Canto XVIII which concerns how the
angry Little People conspired against the Strong Man, Kwasind. And this
canto is followed by a related one, "The Ghosts," which examines
Hiawatha's noble treatment of the dead Indians. The ghosts of the past
come into Hiawatha's view in order that he might warn the living Indians
that they should not be saddened "with useless sorrow" over their own
death (Canto XIX, 174). In Longfellow's imagination of Indian experience,
Indians may lament their extinction, but they should not feel unnecessary
sorrow, for it is useless anyway. Even the dead Indians return from their
world to remind the living Indians of this through Hiawatha. The warning is
well advised for in the next canto, "The Famine" death moves to destroy the
remaining living Indians including Hiawatha's wife, Minnehaha. At the end
of the canto Hiawatha plans his own death, but before he may die his
vision of "The White Man's Foot" and of the coming of the Europeans to the
Indians' land must be told. For Hiawatha, the white men come as friends
and brothers, sent by god, Gitche Manito. Again, in this canto, as in earlier
ones, Longfellow seeks to explain, articulate, and legitimatize the
Europeanization of America; he writes of the "crowded nations" of Europe
and of "restless, struggling, toiling, striving" people "speaking many

tongues, yet feeling but one heart-beat in their bosoms" (Canto XXI, 200-215). That heart-beat is undefined, but its purpose is clear. Then Hiawatha tells of his second vision, a "darker, drearier" one in which the Indians are "scattered," and now they forget Hiawatha's efforts to warn them about their own violence. Consequently, they are "weakened, warring with each other," although no mention of the white men is made in this second vision. Rather Hiawatha sees only death in his image of the Indians as "withered leaves of Autumn" (Canto XXI, 220-29).

In the final canto of the poem, "Hiawatha's Departure," the hero of this revealing cosmic progress has one more vision of exultation. Now devoid of sorrow, he "sees what is to be, but is not" (Canto XXII, 21-28). At this point in the poem Christian imagery is invoked also, as a "Black-Robe," or Christian priest gives Hiawatha the benediction of Christ and Mary and is welcomed into Hiawatha's world. Hiawatha leaves on his own death journey, and in so doing, he reminds his people to "listen to the truth" of the "Black-Robe" (Canto XXII, 192-201). And then Hiawatha moves to his own hereafter, leaving his people in the hands of the white men.

Longfellow designs an American mythology of the Indian and the white man that is peculiarly sensitive to the anxieties and social concerns of a white America rapidly moving across the western wilderness of the Indians' continent. Longfellow solves many problems at once: he explores the violence of the Indians, he reveals them as necessary victims, he justifies white incursions, he idealizes white religious impulses, he even reminds his readers that "useless sorrow" serves no purpose, and he insists that a wilderness populated by whites will bring form and decorum not just to nature but even to the Indians who remain. The poet's design of an Indian cosmic dimension to reveal a reassuring white American political statement is fundamentally comforting to his white audience. Longfellow's calm social vision of the "white man's foot" controlling an Indian chaos provides an implicit source of expiation to white men who feared a turbulent American response to the Indian as well a burdensome American guilt. That same social vision will be turned inside out by Thoreau, quite deliberately. He will employ the same Indian sources and legends to create his own American social vision of ambivalence and quiet desperation The sources of Indian vision in American literature can be read more than one way.

Hawthorne and the Indian

"I have a strange fancy that this brook is the boundary between two worlds." The Scarlet Letter. [41]

For Nathaniel Hawthorne the very physicality of the American wilderness, of life across the "boundary between two worlds," has significance as a source of Indian metaphors of ambivalence and equivocation The keynote of Hawthorne's employment of the Indian is neither longing for the mobility or spirituality of Indian experience, nor a denial of the Indian's savagery, but uneasiness. The intense and possibly destructive possibilities without suggest a potential threat of chaos within. The elemental wildness and wilderness of the Indian exist as a source of purification, but also as a place beyond the boundaries of a moral frame and control.[42]

Images of the Indian as evil representations of the dark heart of mankind are derived from Hawthorne's searches within Puritan experiences for symbols of inner life. This inner life is dark and wild and it engages the individual in quests for identity in a wilderness that nurtures freedom and isolation and the psychological consequences of both.

In The Scarlet Letter Hawthorne interpenetrates the symbolic Indian free and unrestrained, within the experience of Hester Prynne:

> She had wandered, without rule or guidance, in a moral wilderness; as vast, as intricate and shadowy, as the untamed forest, amid the gloom of which they were now

holding colloquy that was to decide their fate. Her intellect and heart had their home, as it were, in desert places, where she roamed as freely as the wild Indian in his woods. For years past she had looked from this estranged position at human institutions, and whatever priests or legislators had established; criticizing all with hardly more reverence than the Indian would feel for the clerical band, the judicial robe, or the church. The tendency of her fate and fortunes had been to set her free.[43]

Here the Indian represents the "estranged point of view" which Hester embraces as her own. The metaphorical "wild Indian" acts as a new lens, a new vision with potential for genuine freedom and for critical acumen not available to those who adhere only to the established institutional orders of church and state, even of the fireside safety of home and family. Hester is alone, isolate and free. Although such freedom and wildness have made her "strong," Hawthorne adds that they have "taught her much amiss"[44] as well. If Hester is deliberately designed as a representative of a "wildness" both appealing and threatening, Dimmesdale acts as a victim of both its attraction and its danger. Hester demands that Dimmesdale respond to the possibilities of wildness:

Whither leads yonder forest track? Backward to the settlement, thou sayest! Yes, but onward, too! Deeper it goes, and deeper, into the wilderness, less plainly to be seen at every step; until, some few miles hence, the yellow leaves will show no vestige of the white man's tread. There thou art free.[45]

The path of liberation that Hester surveys for Dimmesdale and herself is that of the Indian; she finds within it a radical redefinition of inner selfhood. In the Indian's wilderness, man is "free" of restraint, coercion, convention, and the "iron framework" as Hawthorne's describes the "pressure of faith.[46] Yet Dimmesdale ultimately rejects Hester's offer of liberation because he is too rigidly bound to the old order. He is a "true religionist, with the reverential sentiment largely developed, and an order of mind that impelled itself powerfully along the track of a creed."[47] It is the "order of mind" that controls and determines Dimmesdale, it is the "track of a creed" rather than the "forest track" which he follows despite his personal loss. Edwin Fussell observes that the wilderness is the "novel's action."[48] Certainly this is true in the sense that the surrounding forest and Indian trails become a means of signifying the condition of the American in his or her new world. Dimmesdale and Hester each symbolize inherent paths and points of view, variant means of action and adaption, perception and comprehension. At his death Dimmesdale demands, "Is not this better than what we dreamed in the forest?[49] Hawthorne leaves the question deliberately unresolved.

In The Scarlet Letter Hawthorne confronts the idea of freedom and isolation within the American wilderness by attempting to reflect on the essence of vision itself. The Indian represents an "estranged point of view" which becomes Hester's own as well as only means of seeing and surviving. In Hawthorne's version of the American fall he integrates the native figure of the Indian not merely to americanize the text but to provide a revelation of the Indian as primal participant in the relation to the American landscape. The Indian functions as an emblem of Hester's own "forest track" into regions of doubt and freedom, isolation and affirmation of self. It is the track through which she believes Dimmesdale and she might have found some possibility in the "wild, heathen Nature" of the Indian and of the self deep within.[50] It is in the heathen Indian that Hawthorne sees a hint of the nature of vigor and freedom of the forest, which is particularly Hester's and Pearl's terrain. They are quite literally outlaws; their connections with the Indian signify a certain strangeness. The polarities Hawthorne designates between village and frontier, godliness and the heathen, law and freedom serve to distinguish Hester by making of her a women who shares a kind of Indian mode of being. The opposition between Hester and the townspeople cannot be resolved. The essential tension between them points to a more fundamental distinction within the human experience: the opposition between guilt and freedom of will. Hawthorne writes, "But there is still the ruined wall, and near it, the stealthy tread of the foe that would win over again his unforgotten triumph."[51] The triumph of evil can be neither repaired nor ignored. The sense of human ruins, of personal disaster beyond any recompense, save heaven, of spiritual hunger for freedom from guilt which the wild Indian comes to represent, pervades the text. Yet Hawthorne's effort is not merely delineation of unresolvable contrarities, but of the revelation inherent to such creative tension. He seeks nothing less than the full beholding of the meaning of inner wildness and inner order.

Such conflicts, which underscore each of Hawthorne's fictions, are most fully explored in The Scarlet Letter. Melville writes of Hawthorne: "You may be bewitched by his Sunlight transported by the bright gildings in the skies he builds over you; but there is a blackness of darkness beyond.[52] The "blackness beyond" the boundaries of civilization, or worse, within them, together with Hawthorne's belief in the fragility of that civilization reflects an overpowering division. For civilization appears almost defenseless against raids, whether from Indian wildness or moral confusion. Septimius Felton, the unfinished romance, contains onslaughts of both kinds. Septimius, whose origins are derived from the English aristocracty and an American Indian tribe, describes himself:

> That strain of Indian blood is in me yet... and it makes me
> despise,--no, not despise; for I can see their desirableness
> for their people,--but it makes me reject for myself what you
> think is valuable.[53]

Septimius is divided within and without. Whatever path he takes inevitably, "he felt himself strangely ajar with the human race, and would have given much either to be in full accord with it, or separated from it forever."[54] Like his Indian antecedents, Septimius "walks so much the more wildly on his lonely course,"[55] unable ever to resolve the essential conflict of his wildness and consequent loneliness. Finally "crushed and annihilated,"

Septimius escapes to England, and there Hawthorne records "a certain Indian glitter of the eye and cast of feature" in Septimius' progeny.[56] Septimius, the Indian outcast thrust into society, instead of like Hester thrust outside, uncovers and explores the same revealing question: how to cope within a world that seeks to divide and conquer rather than renew and resolve.

Larzer Ziff observes that Hawthorne recognized the implicit didacticism in his writings about the American past.[57] In such figures of the Indian, old legends of Hawthorne's own New England, Hawthorne writes "the very nucleus, the fiction in them, seems to have come out of the heart of man in a way that cannot be imitated by malice afore thought."[58] It is the aesthetic process, the means of revelation that creates "the fiction in them" that Hawthorne searches for so diligently. By using such metaphors as the Indian and his forest track, Hawthorne transforms them into fictions which touch inner experience and societal division. They "come out of the heart of man" because they speak so clearly of that heart within. This transformative vision tells a truth about the essential relation between the American self and the open wilderness. Each American's mode of being is a mere clearing in the forest, surrounded and inter-penetrated by forest tracks and civilized amenities, but nonetheless a place to make and know the self.

NOTES

[1]Anthony F.C. Wallace, The Death and Rebirth of the Seneca (New York, 1970), p. 42.

[2]"Remarks Concerning the Savages of North America," (1784), in The Writings of Benjamin Franklin. Ed. Albert Smyth. (New York, 1907), vol. 10, 97.

[3]Anthony F.C. Wallace, "Cultural Composition of the Handsome Lake Religion," Bulletin, Bureau of American Ethnology, 180 (1961), 139-57.

[4]Weston La Barre, The Ghost Dance. (Garden City, N.Y., 1970), pp. 210-11.

[5]Anthony F.C. Wallace, "The Dakanawidah Myth Analyzed as the Record of a Revitalization Movement," Ethnohistory, 5 (1958), 126.

[6]Gary Nash, Red, White, and Black. (Englewood Cliffs, N.J., 1974), pp 18-19.

[7]Eleanor Wilner, Gathering the Winds. (Baltimore, 1975), pp. 40-41.

[8] Nash, Red, White, and Black, p. 317.

[9] Nash, Red, White, and Black, pp. 318-19.

[10]Tony Tanner, Adultery and the Novel: Contract and Transgression (Baltimore, 1979), pp. 24-27.

[11]Tony Tanner, Adultery and the Novel, p. 26.

[12]Review of James Fenimore Cooper's The Spy, North American Review. Vol. 15. (1821), 255.

[13]Charles Brockden Brown, Edgar Huntly (Philadelphia, 1887), p. 3.

[14]James Fenimore Cooper, Notions of the Americans (London, 1828), II, 142-43.

[15]Nathaniel Hawthorne, "Our Evening Party Among the Mountains," Grandfather's Chair (Boston, 1883), pp. 467-68.

[16]Cooper, Notions of the Americans, 1,328.

[17]Susan Fenimore Cooper, ed., Pages and Pictures from the Writings of James Fenimore Cooper (New York, 1861), pp 129-30.

[18]Susan Fenimore Cooper, Pages and Pictures, pp. 129-30.

[19]Robert Spiller, James Fenimore Cooper: Critic of His Times (New York, 1931), p. 11.

[20]For lucid studies of Leatherstocking and Cooper's wilderness Indians, see Robert Zoeliner's "Conceptual Ambivalence in Cooper's Leatherstocking," American Literature, XXXI (1960), 397-420; John T. Frederick's "Cooper's Eloquent Indians," PMLA, 71 (1956), 1004-17; Joel Porte, The Renance in America (Middletown, 1969), pp. 11-20; and Edwin Fussell's Frontier: American Literature and the American West (Princeton, 1965), pp. 27-68.

[21]Larzer Ziff, Literary Democracy (New York, 1981), pp. 265-66.

[22]James Fenimore Cooper, The Prairie (New York, 1950), p. 69.

[23]Ibid., pp. 1-2.

[24]Ibid., p. 23.

[25]Ibid., pp. 243-44.

[26]Ibid., p. 83.

[27]Ibid., p. 128.

[28]Ibid.

[29]Ibid., p. 289.

[30]Ibid., P. 290.

[31]Ibid.

[32]Ibid., p. 5.

[33]Ibid., p. 452.

[34]Ziff, Literary Democracy, p. 265.

[35]Sacvan Bercovitch, The Puritan Origins of the American Self (New Haven, 1975), p. 234.

[36]Extract from Herman Melville's letter to the Cooper Memorial Committee, Memorial of Cooper (New York, 1853), p. 30.

[37]Henry David Thoreau, A Week on the Concord and Merrimack Rivers (Princeton, 1979), pp. 54-55.

[38]Ernest Moyne quotes from Longfellow's manuscript of "Sketches" in the monograph, Hiawatha and Kalevala (Helsinki, 1963), p. 40.

[39]North American Review, XLV (July, 1837), 34.

[40]Journal (22 June 1854).

[41]Complete Works of Nathaniel Hawthorne. Ed. G.P. Lathrop. (Boston, 1882), V, 208.

[42]For a lucid discussion of the relation between Hawthorne's notion of wildness and Thoreau's, see Frederick Garber, Thoreau's Redemptive Imagination, pp. 71-73.

[43]Works of Nathaniel Hawthorne, V, 239.

[44]Ibid. , V, 240.

[45]Ibid. , V, 242.

[46]Ibid. , V, 151.

[47]Ibid.

[48]Edwin Fussell, Frontier: American Literature and the American West (Princeton, 1965), pp 96-98.

[49]Works of Nathaniel Hawthorne, V, 300.

[50]Ibid., V, 243.

[51]Ibid., V, 241.

[52]Herman Melville, "Hawthorne and His Mosses." The Literary World, VII (17 August 1850), 126.

[53]Nathaniel Hawthorne, Septimius Felton (Boston, 1879), p. 377.

[54]Nathaniel Hawthorne, Septimius Felton, p. 80.

[55]Ibid., p. 81.

[56]Ibid., p. 430.

[57]Larzer Ziff, Literary Democracy (New York, 1981), p. 124.

[58]Nathaniel Hawthorne, Septimius Felton, p. 110.

CHAPTER TWO:
THOREAU AND THE INDIAN

"Wherever I go, I tread in the tracks of the Indian." Henry David Thoreau[1]

For Henry David Thoreau, to tread in the tracks of the Indian is to invoke a symbolic universe. Thus, Thoreau's imagination of the Indian represents not necessarily a return to the tribal world as it actually was, but as it was imagined to have been, a mystification which perfectly fits the need of an American artist searching for an indigenous character to his work. The present study of Thoreau's Indian metaphors reflects on Thoreau's response to the fact of the inevitable extermination of the Indian, as it was perceived by Thoreau's contemporaries, and more proximately, on the role of the imagination in revealing and restoring a fully human and spiritually nutritive vision of man in the figure of the Indian.

When Thoreau writes that "the Indian has vanished as completely as if trodden into the earth, absolutely forgotten except by a few persevering poets,"[2] he is describing his own persevering poetic enterprise. But it is not merely perseverance and memory which mark Thoreau's employment of the Indian. What is immediately striking is the humility and decency with which he approaches the Indian, qualities so remarkable precisely because they are so rare among his American contemporaries. However, Thoreau's noble savage, in so far as he is noble, is so because he possessed qualities that are at variance with those of civilized man. It is this paradoxical difference which was so suggestive to Thoreau's imagination. He refuses to be lost in the chaos of borrowed images and misappellations, but strives instead to reinvent the Indian by going back for materials and beginning again.

The very idea of the Indian can be seen to direct many of Thoreau's activities as well as to reflect his concern with giving account of the quasi-scientific, ethical, racial and linguistical origins of all that surrounds him. The aborigines of America provide a unique means by which Thoreau might "front reality," by getting back to the beginning, by discovering the meaning of the thousands of arrowheads the Indians left behind them. Thoreau's own strenuous effort is to dig to native American culture before it was created in images that had meaning only in relation to a Christian Europe. On many pages of his Journals Thoreau expresses in a striking and decisive fashion what significance might be discovered even in something so small as an arrowhead. On 22 October 1857 he writes of them,

> Such are our antiquities. These were our predecessors. Who then make so great ado about the Roman and the Greek and neglect the Indian? We need not wander off with boys in our imagination to Juan Hernandez to wonder at footprints in the sand there. Here is a print still more significant at our doors, the print of a race that has preceded us, and this little symbol that Nature has transmitted to us. Yes, this arrowhead is probably more ancient than any other, and to my mind it has not been deciphered.[3]

The deciphering of the arrowhead becomes one of Thoreau's inexhaustibly exciting interests. Such deciphering acts are discoveries about what the world was like and ultimately what, as Frederich Garber observes, Thoreau himself is like.[4] In such explorations of the past Thoreau organizes a perception of himself and of his own white world in relation to the Indian's. An Indian arrowhead is not merely an object of discovery, but of consciousness of the past and of the pastness within the present. It is also a metaphor, a "little" symbol of American consciousness discovered and defined. In such a metaphor the Indian's arrowhead is a means of transforming and claiming history through the creative energy of the deciphering artist.

Thoreau is an honorary member of the Boston Society of Natural History to which he leaves at his death "a large series of Indian implements of stone from various parts of New England, but chiefly from the neighborhood of Concord. There were over one hundred specimens of axes, pestles, gouges, mortars, chisels, spear points and ornaments, etc. and a large number of arrowheads of very varied patterns and materials. The entire collection comprises about nine hundred pieces."[5] Thoreau's "Indian Manuscripts" are the written record corresponding to this immense material collection of artifacts. In eleven volumes containing 2,800 handwritten pages Thoreau gathers one of the largest collections of Indian materials from all sources available in the mid-nineteenth century. The process of selection Thoreau employs reveals him to be demanding researcher, critical of authors and concerned with the problem of plagiarism (Thoreau himself identifies his own sources carefully). The extent of his prospective Indian study is evident in the following tentative lists of chapters scribbled on two sheets of paper and slipped in the front cover of the first volume:

My own

Subjects of School-craft's Vol. V

Ante Columbian History
First Aspects of Land and
        People
Welch in America
Traveling
Physiqe
Music
Games
Duelling
Feasting
Food

General History
Manners and Customs
Antiquities
Physical Geography
Tribal Organizations
Intellectual Capacity
Topical History
Physical Type
Language
Art
Conditions and

38

Charity
Funeral Customs
Traditions and History
Morale
Marriage Customs
Manufactures
Education
Dress
Painting
Money
Naming
Government
Treatment of Captives
Manners
Woodcraft
Hunting
Food, etc.
Fishing
Superstition-Religion
Medicine, etc.
War
Language
Indian Relics.
Arts and Uses Derived from Indians

Prospects
Daemoloty, Magic, etc.
Medical Knowledge
Literature and the Ind-
ian Language
Statistics and Popu-
lation
Biography
Religion
Ethnology

Loskiel's Subjects
Origins of Indian Nations
Their Counting
Bodily Constitutions
Character
Languages
Arts and Sciences
Religious Ceremonies and
Superstitions
Dress

Adair's Subjects
Color, Temper and
Dress
Games
Utensils
Manners of Counting
Time
Festivals, Feasts,
and
Religious Rites

Duelling   Laws of Uncleanness
Marriage
Education
Food
Agriculture
Hunting
Fishing
Trade
Traveling
Dancing and other
        Amusements
Diseases and Care
Funerals and Mourning
History Discovery
Political Institutions
Wars and Ceremonies
        attending Peace[6]

In Thoreau's use of the scholarly investigations of Schoolcraft, Loskiel, Adair and many others, the concrete scientific, etymological, racial, and historical distinctions between the white man and the Indian are examined persistently for ideas for a book on the Indians which he never wrote. The extracts and jottings now in the Pierpont Morgan Library are a mass of material so diverse, so contradictory, that it appears no wonder that Thoreau does not ever pull it together into a coherent work. Perhaps he recognizes that the unity he imposed, or tried to impose, on Walden and A Week on the Concord and Merrimack Rivers seems inevitably to elude him. For despite the care and commitment revealed in the list of proposed subjects for his work on the Indian, Thoreau is unable to make full use of his aboriginal materials.

The question of why, given Thoreau's immersion in things Indian, he does not make still more use of the Indian as metaphor or as subject than he does in the writings he does for his own satisfaction is an important one. There are several problems involved: some of the notebooks are written when Thoreau was sick, at least when he seems unable to revive the imaginative fire of his Walden-writing youth. The extracts themselves conform to the demands of a scholarly work, not to the unity of a work of art, and they raise the question of Thoreau's ability to relate to the Indian when not idealized by death or distanced in time.

The notebooks themselves do not provide a simple response to any of the questions they pose. Thoreau's monumental effort of gathering and gleaning cannot be reduced or defined away. There is no single underlying idea of the Indian, but hundreds; there is no continuous stream of narrative, but a series of blocks of quotations from a whole range of sources with little comment from Thoreau himself. The use of a wide range of viewpoints gives moral as well as scientific perspective, offers scope for Thoreau's own imagination, and broadens the sense of the Indian's reality in a world unfriendly to that reality. The multiplicity of variation in style and substance as well as of viewpoint is suggested by a description of the concerns of each volume. In volume one Thoreau searches Thomas Hutchinson's The History of the Colony of Massachusetts Bay (Boston, 1764) and finds that the Indians have "a great fear of death, after all," and discovers, too, something of the Indians' myths about death. In volumes two and three Thoreau investigates Sebastian Rasles' "Early Jesuit Missions" and Daniel Gookin's statistics of Indian population as well as Pierre Francois Xavier de Charlevoix, who in this Journal of a Voyage to North America reflected on the Indians' eloquence "which would have been applauded at Rome and Athens." In volume four Thoreau examines Francis B. Head's The Emigrant (London, 1846); Head makes a distinction between the Indians and the English in material terms and questions how the English would live without "the long list of artificial luxuries which they have been taught to venerate."

Thoreau's process of selection is a careful one that reflects his concern for the Indian as a model of simplification as well as Thoreau's critical perspective on scholars of the Indian. In volumes five and six Thoreau probes Henry Rowe Schoolcraft's History, Condition, and

Prospects of the Indian Tribes of the United States (Philadelphia, 1851-1857) with a skeptical eye which questions why "Schoolcraft did not state distinctly how genuine stories (of 'The Island of the Blessed' and 'The Magic Circle in the Prairie') were and to which tribes they belong," or even where precisely Schoolcraft obtained his sources. Amid such skepticism Thoreau also makes a brief note to himself that the Indians "see the great Spirit in everything." The potentially curative nature of the Indians' mythic imagination whose "ancient history is mythology" discloses a universal human meaning for Thoreau. In volumes seven and eight he appears increasingly interested in the archeological origins of the Indians, so much so that he quotes a report of the American Ethnological Society to the effect that "the monumental evidence is altogether against the hypothesis of a migration from the North, which originated in an overstrained zeal, and which has been perpetuated through ignorance." Volume nine contains a newspaper clipping concerning the Sand Creek Massacre which described a "great battle" between the United States and the Indians. In the final volumes of the notebooks Thoreau studies John Heckewelder's A Narrative of the Missions of the United Brethren among the Delaware and Mohegan Indians, 1740-1808 among (Philadelphia, 1820) with care and several other sources including John Richardson's Arctic Searching Expedition: A Journal of a Boat Voyage through Rupert's Land and the Arctic Sea (New York, 1852). Here Thoreau is particularly concerned with, as he notes, the Indians' "elevation of mind." Heckewelder's belief that the "Indians are proud but not vain, they consider vanity as degrading and unworthy (to) the character of a man" is one estimable trait which is shared by Thoreau not merely in the notebooks but throughout his writings about the Indian.

The notebooks are never to be reshaped into his "own" book about Indians. Thoreau gathers the facts of Indian experience at an astounding rate, particularly during the gestation of Walden. The very size of the "Indian Books" reflects the scope of Thoreau's interest, for they expand from sixty pages to six hundred pages per notebook during the six year period from 1850 to 1856 and then diminish to fewer than two hundred pages annually after 1857. William Howarth observes that as Thoreau's "knowledge grew, his ambition to publish seemed to wane."[7] Certainly Thoreau's ability to apprehend, transmute, and ultimately employ his perceptions in works of art diminishes through the sheer bulk of material. Yet the Indian remains, as a challenge to the imagination, even if unencompassable.

The Indian is the first American; he exists in nature as a part of it, and indeed, is, in Thoreau's mind, a human representative of the natural realm. As a source for Thoreau's imaginative return to the past--a return for spiritual insight and strength--Thoreau turns to the Indian to seek authority for his belief that the only true life is the unencumbered one. By discovering the Indians's "talent for wildness," Thoreau found the means to reempower himself against those as yet unrestored and unfeeling. Thoreau is engaged in an act of redemption; his works are a means of preserving the vestiges of a pre-lapsarian innocence as well as a witness to the destruction of that innocence. As one of those "few persevering poets," he will not have us forget.

Within Thoreau's aesthetic impulse a complex pattern is to be discerned in the metaphorical creations of the Indian. His first work, A Week on the Concord and Merrimack Rivers, is an elegy to a brother who is an unnamed yet vital source of art and feeling,

> Where' ere thou sail'st who sailed with me
> Though now thou climbest loftier mounts,
> And fairer rivers dost ascend,
> Be thou my Muse, my brother --. [8]

It is possible to perceive a sense in which the elegiac expression is transferred from Thoreau's brother, John, to the Indian. Thoreau reminds us to "listen but for an instant to the chaunt of the Indian muse,"[9] thereby drawing a deliberate analogy between the powers of his brother and of the Indian to engender art.

Thoreau's effort here is to listen to the muse in whatever form it takes, but always the very essence of its power in A Week is subsumed in his recognition that the Indian, like his brother, will die. The very nature of the Indian throughout the work is presented in terms of extermination. The first paragraph points to the Indian as an "Extinct race," whose own name for the Concord River, the Musketquid, or Grassground River, has even been lost from the civilized world.[10] Every reference to the Indian places him in the general context of death--the white man "buys the Indian's moccasins and baskets, then buys his hunting grounds, and at length forgets where he is buried and plows up his bones."[11] Thoreau recreates history in the process of telling "of crippled Indians, and their adventures in the woods" while fighting the white man, because "there is no journal to tell them."[12] Even the illustrative example in the panegyric to friendship represents the Indian, Wawatam, and Henry, the fur trader, as characters displacing Henry and John Thoreau. But there, too, the relationship must inevitably end. Wawatam, like Thoreau's brother vanishes so that we "never hear of him again."[13]

The most striking employment of an extended metaphor of extermination is presented in the history of Hannah Dustan, whose account of her captivity Thoreau revises. In his version of the famous narrative, Thoreau makes Mrs. Dustan the key instigator and actor in the extinction of Indians. Mrs. Dustan takes an Indian's tomahawk and scalps her captors in their sleep. The single consequential reference to a woman in all of Thoreau's works of art is to one who kills, in cowardice and savagery, human representatives of the natural realm.

Paradoxically, although the Indians die, the idea of the Indian provides a vital symbol for Thoreau the artist. The death of a beautiful Indian brother, to subvert Poe's crucial theory, serves to shape the imaginative creation of A Week on the Concord and Merrimack Rivers. The metaphor of the Indian both conceals and reveals its origin--it is a strategy of indirection by which the horror of death may be approached and uttered. To express the dark and unsayable, metaphor is required.

Spirituality, fear, and ideal become interpenetrated and then linked with death, for it appears that destruction is inevitable to those who yield themselves up to their full natural potential.

The Indian, although he is being exterminated, offers a unitive and energetic aesthetic vision of power and potential to hold against the fragmented and destructive experience of the white man: "When I consider," Thoreau writes, "that the nobler animals have been exterminated here--the cougar, the panther, lynx, wolverine, wolf, bear, moose, deer, the beaver, the turkey, etc., etc.,I cannot but feel as if I lived in a tamed, and, as it were, emasculated country... Is it not a maimed and imperfect nature that I am conversant with? As if I were to study a tribe of Indians that had lost all of its warriors.."[14] That the Indians have, indeed, lost nearly all their warriors creates in the speaker of A Week a sense of "maimed despair." Only later when awakened and radically transformed by the breaking through of the imagination, is he able to "wish to know an entire heaven and an entire earth."[15]

Thoreau's vision parallels the apocalyptic visions of shaman-prophets who remade their societies in a regenerative assurance of life's primacy even in the midst of an oppressive and life-denying environment. This search for the Indians' metaphorical significance is no longer merely an escape toward their strange, "primitive, rank and savage life," which the Indian also reveals.[16] Thoreau insists that the true eye was not of the mortal body, which will be lost; that man must not seek to escape this knowledge, but to dig into the territory of the Indian to discover the symbols for which the only necessary equipment is spiritual insight. The internal climate is his true home, and the fullest imaginative perception of that landscape can transform the outer world into the forms of harmony discerned within.

The Indian, Thoreau writes in the "Thursday" chapter, is eminently conscious of this inversion in the way the world is usually perceived, and so provides Thoreau with his model spiritual perceiver. In an imaginative reconstitution of the Indian's experience, Thoreau describes the "taking of a scalp" as the way to unleash the imagination and "make a poem." Such a poem is not of a fixed and frozen form of "white man's poetry" and anchored in past time, but is charged with a new vitality.[17] Only by taking a figurative scalp can Thoreau open the cells of the civilized prison of his brain. This is the "other, savager, and more primeval" aspect of experience which is not merely a restatement of primitive possibility as if the other world does not exist, but a creative adaptation to the civilized world. He seeks to preserve the sense of true equilibrium the Indians enjoy between man and nature, which Thoreau searches for at Walden Pond, and at the same time he affirms the ability of the human imagination to take a metaphorical scalp and make the world anew.

In Walden (1854) Thoreau moves beyond elegiac expression of vision of extermination to a joyous celebration of a talent for wildness which will enable him to uncover and unite the chief sources of his art. Here fables, totems, histories and myths function to emphasize the promise offered in man's relation to nature. Every mention of the Indian, even in a seemingly casual description of "the savages' barbarous singing (for they used to sing themselves to sleep)" is artfully manipulated to reveal a double meaning.[18] Not merely does the parenthetical phrase tend to convey a sense of continual rejoicing, even in the Indians' sleep, which was amazing to Winslow and his companions, but it suggests that the Indians were prepared to sing themselves to the final and inevitable sleep of extinction.

Thoreau never supposes that "wildness" is more than an element in his character, and he is a "savage" in only a very special sense, but when he explains his enterprise at Walden Pond he quite naturally reshapes an Indian fable, taken from a world in which he feels thoroughly at home, as a crucial symbol of his work. He tells of a basket weaver who came to town to sell his creations and is dismayed to learn that he would have to create a market for them also, or else make something that white men already wanted to buy. Engaged in a process of identification with the Indian basket weaver and remembering the failure of A Week on the Concord and

46

Merrimack Rivers, Thoreau attempts to learn from the Indian's experience and extends the metaphor to his production: "I too had woven a kind of basket of delicate texture, but I had not made it worth anyone's while to buy them. Yet not the less, in my case, did I think it worth my while to weave them and instead of studying how to make it worth men's while to buy my baskets, I studied rather how to avoid the necessity of selling them."[19] The spiritual lesson learned from the Indian is one of renunciation and celebration in the face of such denial.

In still another strategic digression based on an Indian myth, Thoreau leads us to a conclusion pertinent to this central thesis. His imagination stirs to the latent possibilities of the myth, Thoreau recounts a ritual practised by the Mucclasse Indians: once a year all the Indians' possessions were gathered in a common heap and consumed with fire; this was followed by three days of fasting, then three days of feasting, as the Indians prepared themselves for a new life. Of this purification by fire Thoreau declared: "I have scarcely heard of a truer sacrament, that is, as the dictionary defines it, 'outward and visible sign of inward and spiritual grace.'"[20]

In shaping the facts of the Indian myth, Thoreau fits them to his symbolic use by attaching a multiplicity of meanings relinquishment, joy, religious grace--to the whole. With an instinctive awareness of the significance of myth, he perceives it as an integral, even sacramental, element of the imagination. Neither remote nor rarified, it is "the spirit of humanity, that which animates both so-called savages and civilized nations, working through a man, and not the man expressing himself."[21] While not a savage himself, and much more an artist than a hunter, Thoreau feels in his world no unbridgeable gap between these roles.

In his penetration of the "savage past," Thoreau is not a mythopoeist, in the strict etymological sense of maker of myths; but his imagination achieves its fullest expression in such fabling and mythic narratives where the preternatural or archetypal idea of the Indian is given unity and direction through his artistry. In such fables and myths the Indian becomes a symbolic medium or index for him, a transient entity, to be valued to the degree that it proves instrumental in releasing the spiritual force. Thus, the Indians' rituals of purification through ordeals of fasting and fire represent the universal methods of inducing the mental concentration necessary for the suppression of the conscious mind and for the raising of the unconscious dream world of spirits and the imagination. For Thoreau, the Indian metaphor becomes a means of validating this realm, which discloses itself in vision, and which somehow holds the key to renewed harmony between self and world.

If the function of the artist, as Emerson suggested to his heirs Thoreau and Whitman, is always to renew the primitive and spiritual experience of the race, so that man "still goes back for materials and begins again on the most advanced stage,"[22] then Thoreau's talent for wildness is far more than eccentricity or playfulness. The Indian provides a rich source of human archetypes, which are never autonomous but always interpenetrated with the wildness of the surrounding woods and fields of Thoreau's imagination. It is the wildness which Thoreau ferrets beneath the merely conscious levels of cultivated man, in undebauched Indians, and in the realm of tooth and claw, that heartens us by its seemingly inexhaustible vitality and gives us the promise of a kind of inward renewal if we will only search carefully enough.

A search of Ralph Waldo Emerson's own efforts to renew the primitive and spiritual experience through a discovery of the Indian leads us on a somewhat meandering course. For although he wrote in his Journals that "the Indians have a right to exist in this world; they are, (like Monadnoc and the Ocean), a part of it, and fit the other parts,"[23] Emerson also appears able to accept the extinction of the Indian as inevitable: "He is overpowered by the gaze of the white, and his eye sinks."[24] Even Emerson's famous statement of protest to President Van Buren concerning the removal of the Cherokees, an agrarian and literate tribal group-- "The soul of man, the justice, the mercy that is the heart's heart in all men, from Maine to Georgia, does abhor this business"[25]--appears written under the influence of Charles Emerson and is sent too late to have much effect. Emerson's correspondence reveals the half joking manner with which he regarded Thoreau's concern with things Indian.   For example, in a biographical sketch of Thoreau, Emerson recalled how Thoreau charges "a youth setting out for the Rocky Mountains to find an Indian who could tell the secret of the making of stone arrowheads."[26] The youth was Edward Waldo Emerson, and his father, Ralph Waldo Emerson, suggests humorously that his son carry "an arrowhead in your pocket, to hold it up to every Indian you meet, and have Mr. Thoreau answered."[27]

To search Walden for the hidden invitation of the Indian is like decoding a message or secret which contains a promise.   For there Thoreau demonstrates what Emerson merely observes.   In the chapter "Brute Neighbors," Thoreau describes the elusive nature of the pursuit and of the pursuer who seek to drive wild life into his corner for closer observation, through the tale of "a pretty game, played on the smooth surface of the pond, a man against a loon."[28] To hazard the world of the loon Thoreau enters a territory where the resources of nature, captured in the totemic figure of the loon, allowed him to make a journey in the inner world. A sentence cancelled from the first version of this chapter reinforces this idea: "There is always a wild and yet wilder life somewhere sustaining itself at any moment that we allow for, which corresponds to the rareness of some of our thoughts."[29] Excised perhaps because of the too obvious nature of the statement of an idea Thoreau hopes to convey by more subtle means, the sentence is nonetheless helpful in that it acts as a gloss on the concept of wildness and on Thoreau's moment of rendezvous with the loon.

Our introduction to the totem bird, conceived as a heavenly messenger by many Indian tribes with whom Thoreau is acquainted, is scientific and deceptive in tone:

In the fall the loon (Colymbus glacialis) came, as usual, to
moult and bathe in the pond, making the woods ring with his
laughter... Each time, when he came to the surface, turning
his head this way and that, he coolly surveyed the water and
the land, and apparently chose his course so that he might
come up where there was the greatest distance from the
boat. It was surprising how quickly he made up his mind and
put his resolve into execution. He led me at once to the
widest part of the pond, and could not be driven from it.
While he was thinking one thing in his brain, I was
endeavoring to divine his thought in mine.[30]

The paragraph moves as Thoreau does from the mundane known and
scientifically classifiable to the transcendental knowable and back again.
Thoreau recapitulates an archetypal theme; that of man's desire to effect a
human connection with the animal world as a means of spiritual rebirth.
Here in the passage, the human and the animal become deliberately
confused in the consistent use of "he," as the loon was anthropomorphized
into a creator and guide, who in some undestroyed and even nutritive
sense, is a specialist in the divine, peculiarly able to know man and lead
them to spiritual redemption.

Thoreau's need for a figure capable of helping him to imagine such
a redemption leads him to discover loons and Indians as he hazards his
own inner journeys. In looning, a kind of spiritual lunacy, Thoreau also
recognizes that to venture within is to enter a milieu where one may fail,
might finally exhaust the resources that allowed one to make the journey,
that in fact it cannot be prolonged indefinitely, that the destruction of the
natural world, whether in the form of loon or Indian, and the return of
civilization is inevitable. As Thoreau puts it, "I left him disappearing far
away on the tumultuous surface."[31]

Thoreau keeps himself from falling into the delusion that he wishes
actually to become either loon or Indian. But his perception of the

"unhandselled savage nature,"[32] is reinforced with such energy that it is able to create a bridge of metaphor that carries across from one mode of existence to another. Only by discovering such metaphors can the artist disclose the actual complexity of inner experience and reveal the potential meaning of the aesthetic experience, for they become the things commensurate with our American need for wonder about the Indian. Fulfulling an almost shamanistic function as a diviner, his visionary and dissociative powers enable him to act out the conflicts of a socially and racially afflicted America, so that in his vision it may be restored. Through a combination of intuitive insight and careful observation of such things as the movement of a loon, Thoreau dramatizes the disequilibrium between man and the natural world and employs the techniques of his art to reduce it, not the least of which is the dramatization itself. Seeking to make an unknown visible and palpable by giving it shape and form, he adds to the mythological store of his own culture in these original variations on the myths and themes of the Indian. Thoreau's personalized creations of the world of the spirits, of a parallel realm of gods and natural ancestors, invite us to conclude that by seeking out the Indian, we may find a figure to illuminate the mystery of that realm, and seek him out Thoreau did.

Even in the "narrow shelf-like path" around Walden Pond, Thoreau discovers a metaphor, which like a natural living thing is not fixed or permanent, but the result of a process of creation.[33] For Thoreau, the Indian, and all who find their way around the pond participate in the making of the path. "In the steep hill-side, alternately rising and falling, approaching and receding from the water's edge, as old probably as the race of man here, worn by the feet of aboriginal hunters, and still from time to time unwittingly trodden by the present occupants of the land,"[34] its function and order appear invulnerable to human desecration. This is partly because the presence of the path is perceived only by "one standing on the middle of the pond in winter, just after a light snow has fallen, appearing as a clear undulating white line, unobscured by woods and twigs, and very obvious a quarter of a mile off in many places where in summer it is hardly distinguishable close at hand."[35] Thoreau's ability to decode the still hidden messages of the Indian provide a defense not only of the Indian, but of the inner life of man, of what is unseen but truly present, and even of the imagination itself, which is in this metaphor printed by the snow in "clear white type alto-relievo."[36]   To Thoreau's contemporaries who will destroy the Indian and divide themselves in order to conquer, he creates the possibility of a visionary grammar of the inner realm, written for all to see, if they will only look for it.

Even the Indian's wildness, for all that Thoreau cherishes a strain of it in himself and others, is found insufficient in itself. He never proposes that we should dispense with all the accoutrements of civilization, much less with its intellectual refinements.   In fact he employs those very refinements in order to preserve what little remains of that wildness in his works of art.   Surrounded by the rewards of joy, freedom, celebration, spirituality, and even the possibilities of the imagination, the figures of wildness prove that one needs to serve the institutions of civilization in order to be honored by them, that the inner realm truly does exist, and finally that its terrain, if lonely and strange, is also rich and creative.

From Walden Thoreau moves in a different direction entirely. He studies the Indian in a scholarly fashion and presents his findings in the form of travel literature. In a conscious attempt at journalistic jocosity, Thoreau recreates a guided excursion through the wilderness with his Indian guides, Joe Atteion and Joe Polis. Not sentimentally idealistic, but sanely realistic though withal sympathetic in its treatment of the Indian, the world could be seen as a kind of "Indian Notebook" in polished form. There are several problems in using the essays of The Maine Woods (1864): they are written when Thoreau was sick and needed money; they conform to the conventions of the magazine travel article, not to the unity he shaped in Walden and tried to discover in A Week on the Concord and Merrimack Rivers; and they raise the question of Thoreau's ability to relate to the Indian not as a figure imagined, but one rude and close at hand. Through such close contact Thoreau seeks to reach an audience much wider than that measured by the literary community, one for which the Indian and his world held interest and could be made to feel more. It is not so surprising then that the chapters of The Maine Woods and other travel pieces Thoreau published in magazines provide him with an audience he had never had before, and that they help keep not merely the memory of the Indian alive, but that of Thoreau as well.[37]

In the essays, the opposing yet complementary ideas of wildness and civilization, notions central to Thoreau's use of the Indian in A Week and Walden, form the central focus of The Maine Woods. Robert Sayre has suggested that The Maine Woods is "unquestionably his most important book about the Indian, his (own) book about Indians which he did write."[38] While any case for a book about Indians is moot, The Maine Woods is a guide and stimulus to the study of the natural history and the Indians in Maine.

Always in these essays we are reminded of the uncompromising nature of Thoreau's calling as an artist intent on creating a symbolic universe. His retirement into Indian studies, like the retirement to Walden Pond, is a gesture, and one which becomes a symbol. How important it was to reaffirm the metaphorical nature of the Indian in America in which The Maine Woods is shaped can be corroborated by the search that was being made by another persistent explorer during the eighteen-fifties, Herman Melville. Although the symbols of the primitive speak with different meanings to Melville than they do to Thoreau, the two articles share an instinctive awareness of their significance. In The Maine Woods Thoreau senses too the destructive quality of the civilized mind if by its criticism of the savage it serves merely to divorce man from his past by reducing it to a remote stage of human racial development. Beyond the bright circle of the white man's educated consciousness are unsuspected energies that are "not the invention of historians and poets," but a "purely wild and primitive American sound." Thoreau writes, "I felt that I stood, or rather lay, as near to the primitive man of America, that night, as any of its discoverers ever did."[39] In these woods Thoreau is dealing not with archaeological finds, but with real live Indians, though to be sure partly changed by contact with whites. When camping with the Indians Thoreau and his party feel they had to spread blankets over the natives' hides, "so as not to touch them anywhere."[40] Amid the dirt and change and deterioration Thoreau discovers in their way of life, Thoreau observes that "though I had found so many arrowheads" the unaltered Abenaki language "took me by surprise."[41] Eating moosemeat in the rude camp on the Penobscot River appears not quite to fulfil the transcendental urge to be at one with nature and redeem the soul from materialism. The Indians themselves have become "spectulators in moosehides" and do as they "had been taught by the whites."[42] These not so estimable qualities, from Thoreau's point of view, are mitigated by admirable elements in the Indians' character and way of life Thoreau finds as he comes to know his Indian guides, Joe Atteion and Joe Polis, more intimately.

Thoreau responds to these Indians as men, discovering in physical and mental competition with them a satisfying, if somewhat skeptical, relationship. With them, Thoreau, always before the tutor, now becomes a rather clumsy student, anxious to learn woodcraft from experts, and at the same time eager to show his own prowess under the most difficult circumstances. In the race between Joe Polis and Thoreau over the carry there is a competitive, but gently lighthearted show of their friendship as the two men chase each other through the woods. Thoreau, carrying the many small bundles of the camp, reaches the end first, but refuses to "mention this as anything of a feat, for it was but poor running on my part." Polis, bearing the canoe, seems delighted with his game as he told Thoreau, "Locks (rocks) cut 'em feet," and laughingly adds, "Oh, me love to play sometimes."[43] It is as if the pretty game played against the loon now has been fully humanized. Thoreau hazards the real world of the Indian and discovers there a territory where the resources of nature allow him to make a journey, not so much of redemption in the inner world, but of connection and delight in the outer one.

In this milieu Thoreau appears unable to allow himself to fail to find some other form of spiritual resource. His exultation at seeing phosphorescent wood for the first time "could have hardly have thrilled me more if it had taken the form of letters, or of the human face." The strange phenomenon of "light that dwells in rotten wood" reveals to Thoreau "that there was something to be seen if one had eyes. It made a believer of me more than before. I believed that the woods were not tenantless, but chockfull of honest spirits as good as myself any day."[44] His pleasure in the light, which was used by Indian jugglers and shamans to amaze their people--they pretended to hold coals of fire in their mouths--possesses the quality of a revelation. But Thoreau finds humor too in knowing that not only was it "excellent," but also "that it was so cheap."[45] For all its apparent cheapness, Thoreau finds in its light a quality of the pastness of the present, of the Indian's illimitable extension backward to the roots of American history. After making its acquaintance he demands, "Where is all your knowledge gone to?"[46] The possibility that the knowledge of the civilized may go the same path as the Indian, that Thoreau himself may ultimately exhaust the energies that allowed him to make his imaginative journeys, and that the venture itself may be lost to defeat and death is a real one. When first entering the preconscious and unknown realm of the Indian he discovers in phosphorescent wood a belief that although the destruction of the Indian was inevitable, its radiance might redeem life. But later he told us, "I kept those little chips and wet them again the next night, but they emitted no light."[47] Thus, The Maine Woods is a continuation of Thoreau's effort to comprehend and harmonize the dilemma he perceives in the white man's relation to the American wilderness and the American Indian.[48]

To Thoreau the importance of the metaphor of the Indian is in part in the fact that it involves certain acts which, however unspectacularly scholarly or difficult, are nevertheless visible and concrete attempts to put into some actual practice theories which could not honorably be allowed to remain theories. Emerson may talk about breaking conventions over them, but there is nothing in his outward way of life capable of shocking the most conventional. Thoreau, on the other hand, is determined to take some step. To this end he becomes an elegist meditating upon the extinction of the Indian, a scholar of Indian lore and history, a man who finds spiritual experience while being lost in the mazes of the natural realm, an artist who recovers a chief source of his own art in his imagination of the Indian. It is given that the metaphorical Indian is not the only redemptive trope in Thoreau's mind--he possesses multitudes--, that he is unable to make full use of the aboriginal materials in the notebooks because of their complexity and lack of unity, and that eating moosemeat in a camp on the Penobscot cannot quite redeem the soul. Still in the process of his creation Thoreau brings the Indian into the light and in so doing he forges a unique imagination of the Indian.

NOTES

[1] Henry David Thoreau, The Journals of Henry David Thoreau. Eds. Bradford Torrey and Francis Allen (19 March 1842), I, 337.

[2] Henry David Thoreau. The First and Last Journeys of Thoreau. Ed. Franklin B. Sanborn. (Boston, 1905), I, 36.

[3] Henry David Thoreau, The Writings of Henry David Thoreau (Boston, 1906), X, 118.

[4] Frederick Garber, Thoreau's Redemptive Imagination (New York, 1977), p. 11.

[5] Third Annual Report of the Trustees of the Peabody Museum of American Archaeology and Ethnology. (Boston, 1870), pp. 6-7. These materials are held by the Peabody Museum of Harvard University, Cambridge, Massachusetts.

[6] The lists of subjects and the manuscript notebooks are in the Pierpont Morgan Library, New York, New York. Schoolcraft's Vol. V refers to his History, Condition, and Prospects of the Indian Tribes of the United States (Philadelphia, 1851-1857); George Henry Loskiel's subjects are taken from chapter headings of his History of the Mission of the United Brethren among the Indians in North America (London, 1794); and James Adair's subjects are derived from his History of the American Indians (London, 1775).

[7] William Howarth, The Literary Manuscripts of Henry David Thoreau (Columbus, Ohio, 1974), pp. 294-95.

[8] Henry David Thoreau, A Week on the Concord and Merrimack Rivers, Walden Edition. (Boston, 1906), the first epigram, unpaginated.

[9] Thoreau, A Week, pp 63-64.

[10] Ibid., p. 3.

[11] Ibid., p. 61.

[12] Ibid., p. 146.

[13] Ibid., pp. 342-44.

[14] Ibid., p. 63.

[15] Ibid., p. 63.

[16] Henry David Thoreau, Walden. Ed. J. Lyndon Shanley. (Princeton, N.J. 1971), p. 210.

[17] Thoreau, A Week, pp. 60-63.

[18]Thoreau, Walden, p. 143.

[19]Ibid., p. 19.

[20]Ibid., p. 58.

[21]Passage quoted by F.O. Matthiessen in American Renaissance (New York, 1941), p. 648.

[22]Emerson is quoted by F.O. Matthiessen in American Renaissance, p. 174.

[23]Ralph Waldo Emerson, The Journals and Miscellaneous Notebooks of Ralph Waldo Emerson. Eds. Ralph Orth and Alfred Ferguson. (Cambridge, Mass., 1971), IX, (1846), 400.

[24]Ralph Waldo Emerson, "Civilization," The Writings of Ralph Waldo Emerson. VII, 20.

[25]Emerson, Writings, II 89-96.

[26]Ibid., X 473.

[27]Ralph Rusk, ed., The Letters of Ralph Waldo Emerson (New York, 1937), pp. 278-79.

[28]Thoreau, Walden, p. 235.

[29]J. Lyndon Shanley, The Making of Walden (Chicago, 1957), p. 192.

[30]Thoreau, Walden, pp 233-235.

[31]Ibid., p. 236.

[32]Emerson, "The American Scholar," Writings, pp. 99-100.

[33]Thoreau, Walden, p. 180.

[34]Ibid.

[35]Ibid.

[36]Ibid.

[37]Joseph Wood Krutch, Henry David Thoreau (New York, 1947), pp. 250-51.

[38]Robert Sayre, Thoreau and the American Indian, p.155.

[39]Henry David Thoreau, The Maine Woods. Ed. Joseph J. Moldenhauer. (Princeton, N.J., 1972), p. 137.

[40]Ibid., p.135.

[41]Ibid., p. 136.

58

[42]Ibid., pp. 137-82.

[43]Ibid., pp. 285-86.

[44]Ibid.,180-82.

[45]Ibid., p. 181.

[46]Ibid., p. 182.

[47]Ibid.

[48]Philip F. Gura in "Thoreau's Maine Woods Indians: More Representative Men," American Literature (November, 1977), 366-84, sees Thoreau's Indian as an "example of what virtues Americans needed to retain significance in their lives."

[49]See also Robert Sayre, Thoreau and the American Indians, especially pp. 63-69, and 213-15, for additional evidence in support of this point of view.

CHAPTER THREE:
MELVILLE AND THE INDIAN

"The Indians do sorely abound."[1]

The writings of Herman Melville reveal a vision of the Indian that is symbolic and organic, even rather haphazard, but is also consistent with his definition of reality.[2] Melville recognizes that man and his creations are irrational composites, and thus, the metaphorical Indian represents all the violent divisions which threaten the life of man with its own destruction, as well as an image of radiant health, of imagination itself, which helps to illuminate the despair of the white man. Melville, in his reflections on the Indian, employs a method of creation that is not only suggestive of the confusion and inscrutability endemic to the white man's relation with the Indian, but one in which something new and elemental appears. Through his compassionate and exploratory representations of the Indian, we cannot help seeing to what extent Melville perceives the varying ways that white and Indian experience are inextricably mingled and share an inherent savagery as well as a common possibility for regeneration. Beneath the surface conflicts and, indeed, through them, Melville gives many sides of the situation--hence his metaphorical creation of both good and bad Indians, the good side of bad Indians, and the bad side of good Indians, Indians sinned against and Indians sinning.

Melville, himself, experiences the physical world of the Indian at fairly close proximity, and he also knows the Indian as expressed in the sources of popular and folk culture, in history, in travel literature, and in the literary works of his American contemporaries, but always he attempts to reinterpret his sources, to give his own version of the Indian based on his own experience of their way of life.

In 1840, Melville, in a voyage through the Great Lakes, travels to the West. The genuine American wilderness at that time began with Lake

Huron, and for Melville the journey is rich in associations to the American Indian. Approaching Mackinac Island, he saw the wigwams of the Indians (Objibways, Menominees and Winnebagos) summering on the beach. His trip included a rather conventional excursion to the Falls of Saint Anthony in Minnesota, where like many others, he notes the misery of the Indians there.[3] Memories of his western travels are reflected throughout the Melville canon, as recollections transformed into fanciful allusions that will be blended with his later journeys to Polynesia and as reflections of his fundamental compassion for all victims of oppression.

Melville's most explicit statement of "dissent," as he put it, against the traditional treatment of the Indian in America occurs in his review of Francis Parkman's The California and Oregon Trail (1849). There Melville firmly rejects Parkman's belief that the "slaughter of an Indian is as indifferent as the slaughter of a buffalo."[4] Melville tells us that Parkman's work is one for those who wish to "quit Broadway" and penetrate "only in fancy" to the "Lands of the Moccasins,...the region of wampum and calumet." Melville's contempt for the indifference of Parkman, and his compassion for the human remnants of the "Land of Moccasins" is clear, for, he writes, "we are all of us--Anglo-Saxon, Dyaks, and Indians sprung from one head, and made in one image. And if we regret this brotherhood now, we shall be forced to join hands hereafter.. The savage is born a savage; and the civilized being but inherits his civilization, nothing more. Let us not disdain, then, but pity."[5]

The mythic and artistic store of the Indian runs the gamut of imaginative metaphors for Melville, reflecting not only his sense of the Indians' way of peace, their relation to the natural order and their social connections within the tribe, but also his awareness of the disorder, disharmony and destruction wrought by the white men. For example, Melville dwells in the review on a favorite image of the red men smoking "Indian pipes," which later he would transform into a "tomahawk-pipe" in Moby-Dick. By attaching an ominous connotation, through repeated associations of the pipe with ideas of both Pacifism and bellicosity, he signals, literally and metaphorically, disaster as well as hope in the figure of the Indian. Melville's assertion of the universal brotherhood of mankind, explicitly stated here, will be repeated directly in the "Monkey-Rope" chapter of Moby-Dick. There the Anglo-Saxon, Ishmael and Queequeg, are "forced to join hands" in order to survive.[6] The metaphor of joined hands reflects, too, Melville's concern with man's original tragedy, his fall and separation from innocence from his true self. Here it is accompanied by the promise of reunification through the heroic appearance of the Indian, so that together white men and red men may be seen to restore the connections between the divided realms of their experience.

A tomahawk-pipe, such as the one Queequeg carried, decorates the great fireplace of the Melville family home in the Berkshires, where Moby-Dick is written. Other relics of the Indian find their way into the homestead, "Arrowhead," named for the mementoes Melville collects and gathers around him from his travels. The Polynesian-Indian analogy, which Melville initiates in the South Sea narratives Typee and Omoo, and which he develops fully in the characterization of Queequeg in Moby-Dick, appears derived from the anthropological speculations of a friend of Melville's, Alexander Bradford, whose treatise, American Antiquities and Researches into the Origins and History of the Red Race posits a Pacific Ocean origin for the American Indian.[7] For Bradford, "The red race, under various modifications, may be traced physically into many countries, including "Polynesia and America." Evidence for the intermingling of Polynesian and Indian culture, found by Bradford, is used by Melville also. For example, Bradford believes that these two diverse cultures are related in their common creation of "hieroglyphic paintings." Bradford also notes that the "form of the pipe on the tomahawk of the natives of the South Sea islands... all approximate those people to the American aborigines."[8] Artifacts and hieroglyphic painting and the tattoo, together with the associations of the ideas Melville gleaned from his own travels to the West and to Polynesia, made the identification, literally and metaphorically, a source of art as well as anthropology.

For Melville the quest of western civilization in its voyages across the seas and its confrontations with native populations further relate the experience of the Polynesian to the American Indian. In Typee the narrator quite naturally makes a metaphorical connection between the Marquesans and the Indians as he probes the issue of civilization:

> The voluptuous Indian, with every desire supplied, whom Providence has bountifully provided with all the sources of pure and natural enjoyment, and from whom are removed so many of the ills and pains of life--what has he to desire at the hands of Civilization?... Let the now diseased, starving, and dying natives answer the question.[9]

By a process of natural association Melville transforms his Polynesian characters into American Indians and suggests that they, too, may share a common fate,

> Let the savages be civilized, but civilize them with benefits, and not with evils. The Anglo-Saxon have extirpated Paganism from the greater part of the North American continent; but with it they have likewise extirpated the greater portion of the red race.[10]

Melville's presentation of the Indian in the Polynesian context of Typee may be vague in its sense of location, but the implications beneath the analogy are clear: as the Indians have been extinguished, so will the Polynesians as well.

In Typee the despoiling of another New World is recreated in microcosm with the characters, Toby and Tommo, acting as explorers. Their invasion of the Marquesas, as yet untainted by contact with western civilization, becomes suggestive of the archetypal American experience. Tommo, the narrator of Typee, rejects his "errand in the wilderness--a wilderness which already belongs to "wild savages," when he escapes the intellectually limiting captivity of the islanders. Thus, while Typee is chiefly a defense of the unspoiled primitivism Melville himself encountered during his brief residence in Typee Valley in July and August, 1842,[11] it also contains elements of the Captivity Narrative. Like all such narratives this one has a clearly didactic as well as an entertaining purpose, but Melville's is not the typical message of suffering and spiritual transformation of the victim. Melville calls for the rejection of the primitivists' uncritical acceptance of the "savage" and more comprehensively, of what appears to Melville as an almost mindless "savage" existence, but he rejects also the whites' uncritical insistence that all cultures conform to a single standard.[12]

Melville concludes that the actual complexity of the social and religious systems of the Marquesas, or, indeed, of any alien system are not easily understood or categorized. Tommo tells his readers that the Marquesan religious custom of what might be cannibalism "altogether passed my comprehension. Mehevi sought to enlighten my ignorance, but he failed as signally as when he had endeavored to initiate me into the perplexing arcana of the taboo."[13] The only consistent pattern to be discerned is the violence with which the narrative inevitably concluded. About that there could be no confusion: the only form of resolution possible following confrontation with whites is death. Tommo, who unwittingly destroyed the peace of the Typees by his very presence, is almost killed by a Polynesian with "his tomahawk between his teeth," in short, by an American Indian weapon. Even here a fundamental ambivalence pervades the narrative as Mow-Mow, whose tomahawk, in effect, makes him an Indian, is brutally struck in self-defense by the white man who felt "horror at the act," but has "no time for pity or compunction," in his desperate effort to escape the Typees.[14]

Mow-Mow and other less than idyllic savages, like the mysterious "goblin-friend" who appeared in Omoo, along with the infinitely desirable Fayaway and devoted Kory-Kory, make up a composite metaphorical

64

world of Polynesian-Indians. The ambiguous elements contained within the nature of their origins or the manner of their character constantly recur in Melville's response to the Indian. In his invocation of the Indian as a force of man's deepest past, Melville's images rise to sustain and renew his early interest in the native, and allow him to move far beyond the fairly simple ambivalence inherent to the presentation of the Polynesian-Indian in Typee.

When the natural order of a native culture is destroyed by white men, the consequence, as in Typee, is strife. White-Jacket expresses this "man of war world" where the puns and allusions to Indians are consistently martial, corresponding to the "man of war theme. For example, when the narrator speaks of some "rather gentlemanly private, native-born American, who had served in the Seminole campaigns of Florida,"[15] he not only creates an ambiguity in the phrase "native-born American" which opened to speculation the question of who are genuine native Americans, but reminds his readers of particularly bloody Seminole wars in which the United States resorted to flagrant dishonesty--in the capture of Oceola, in the burning of Indian villages and the seizure of Spanish-controlled territories--in dealing with the Indians. In the characterization of Red Hot Coal, who, like the Seminoles, is one of the victims of a "national selfishness (that) is unbounded philanthropy,"[16] Melville designs a demonic "bloodthirsty savage" who was as spiteful as he was repulsive. In the description of the Indian's blanket on which bloody hands are painted as symbolic trophies of scalped foes, the narrator's tone becomes compassionate in its despair over all men's inhumanity. He equates the sinking of the American frigate, Macedonia, to "two bloody red hands painted on the poor savage's blanket," and demands "are there no Moravians on the moon, that not a missionary has yet visited this poor pagan planet of ours, to civilize civilization and christianize Christians?"[17]

It is at this extreme that the vision of such a "missionary" comes--to an exceptional individual whose personal plight mirrored that of "this poor pagan planet," in that he is himself suicidal, beset by sorrows, deprivation, and feelings of hopelessness--in the novel which follows White-Jacket, Moby-Dick. There the Polynesian-Indian, Queequeg appears as the personification of creative force and sensuous experience, sweeping aside the white Ishmael's old and chronic complaints and shaping a new, if temporary, sense of unity between them. The Amerindian prophet Handsome Lake provides a case in point. According to Anthony Wallace, such "vision experience per se is not psychopathological but rather the reverse, being a synthesizing and often therapeutic process performed under extreme stress."[18] Then the individual imagination becomes the crucible for the vision which responds to an attempt to resolve what was also a collective crisis.[19] Thus, Ishmael, who at first finds himself "involuntarily pausing before coffin warehouses, and bringing up the rear of every funeral," discovers that losing all hope is the first step in finding it.[20]

A crucial element inherent in Melville's metaphorical Indians and also to the relationship between Ishmael and Queequeg is the expression of feelings, feelings long suppressed or forbidden by white men. It is partly the upsurge of these feelings, whether violent or loving or both, which permits the rites of Queequeg's diety, Yojo, to be seen as curative in and of themselves:

> So I kindled the shavings; helped prop up the innocent little idol; offered him burnt biscuit with Queequeg, salaamed before him twice or thrice; kissed his nose; and that done, we undressed and went to bed, at peace with our own consciences and all the world.[21]

What matters here for Ishmael is the rite and vision which allow him to come into contact with feelings whose cruelty come essentially from being denied. The result for Ishmael's hypo-ridden soul is union rather than disunion. Ishmael speaks of the "ice of indifference" between himself and Queequeg, and indeed, all men, which "soon thawed" under the pagan warmth of the native's heart: "I felt a melting in me."[22] Queequeg' sactions permit a transcendence of Ishmael's "splintered" self that puts him back into touch with the deeper levels of his own being and with others. It is this, together with the fact that the ritual itself makes him feel that he is the active agent of his own destiny, which constitutes the emotionally healing gift of the Polynesian-Indian's good spirits.

Melville depicts a struggle between two levels of existence: the spiritual, healing one symbolized by Queequeg and the tragic, splintered one, like our own world, that is characterized by Ahab. But it is, of course, the world of the metaphorical Indian in all its diversity and in its contrasting relation to Ahab's realm that requires further examination here. Melville portrays Tashtego, a Gay Head Indian from Nantucket, and Queequeg, as natives equipped with the characteristic implements of the American Indian. Tashtego reveals the "daring" and "wild strength" of the native warrior, and it is he who unconsciously imparts the mystery of the Town-Ho in his sleep. But it is Queequeg who acts as the most significant spokesman of the Indian theme by establishing momentarily a world of feeling in the teeth of tragic opposition. He becomes the spiritual and creative agent of Ishmael's rebirth.

It is Queequeg, too, who reveals in the symbolic resonances of his tattooed body the functioning of the imagination. His own body contains in the various hieroglyphic figures a metaphor of the mind and body joined through the means of the visionary imagination. These tattoos, covering virtually all the Polynesian-Indian's person, are "the work of a departed prophet or seer of his island, who by these hieroglyphic marks, had written out on (Queequeg's) body a complete theory of the heavens and earth, and a mystical treatise on the art of attaining truth."[23] Queequeg's tattooes achieve universal meaning, as the "living parchment" of Queequeg's own self becomes a work of art. The meaning of art and the truth of existence incised upon a man's living body in the cuneiform language of a "departed" culture is a further extension of the metaphorical affirmation of Queequeg's ability to thrust beyond spatial and temporal limitations. Queequeg spends "Many spare hours... in carving the coffin lid with all manner of grotesque figures and drawings; and it seemed that thereby he was striving, in his rude way, to copy parts of the twisted tattooing of his body."[24] His approaching death then is not an end in itself, but an "endless end,"[25] one that provides a springboard for the imagination of Ishmael. In Queequeg's "rising with great force," Melville divulges the aesthetic impulse contained within the cannibal's transcendent act.

As affirmative qualities accrued to Queequeg's symbolic nature, Melville suggests in the native's fearless response to death, the nature of the chiliast living in the universe of his feelings quite directly, and it is this which accounts for his constant hope, not experienced as a remote idea, but as a living force at work in the world. The two Indians on the sea-frontier of the Pequod are related metaphorically through an act of life-giving that foreshadowed Queequeg's deliverance of Ishmael. The saving of Tashtego, like Queequeg's other rescues, is a spontaneous action in harmony with natural process. The Gayhead Indian "like the twin reciprocating bucket in a veritable well, dropped head-foremost down into this great Tun of Heidelburg, and with a horrible oily gurgling, went clean out of sight.'" But Queequeg takes "poor, buried-alive Tashtego" out of danger, and through "the courage and great skill in obstetrics of Queequeg, the deliverance, or rather, delivery of Tashtego, was successfully accomplished."[26] Death, Ishmael learns, is not something inflicted, a visitation in which men take only a passive part and against which they must resist violently; but it is a natural and inevitable part of the process of life, inextricably related here to metaphors of birth. If all men carry the fact of their own death with them, few are like Queequeg, almost comfortable with the burden they must bear: [27]

> Then crossing his arms on his breast with Yojo between, he called for the coffin lid... to be placed over him. The head part turned over with a leather hinge, and there lay Queequeg in his coffin with little but his composed countenance in view. "Rarmai" (it will do; it is easy), he murmured at last, and sighed to be replaced in his hammock.[28]

Queequeg appears able to exert total control over the processes of life and death and simply decides that death could be postponed for a more appropriate moment:

> ...the cause of his sudden convalescence was this;--at a critical moment, he had just recalled a little duty ashore, which he was leaving undone; and therefore had changed his mind about dying; he could not die yet, he averred. They asked him, then whether to dive or die was a matter of his own sovereign will and pleasure. He answered, certainly.[29]

A sequence of death and rebirth must be reenacted again and again for Ishmael fully to comprehend its meaning. Just as earlier Queequeg practices obstetrical skills on the other Indian on the Pequod, the Gayhead, Tashtego, and accomplishes his "deliverance, or rather, his delivery,"[30] so finally, it is Queequeg who keeps Ishmael afloat for "almost one whole day and night" after the Pequod has been destroyed.[31] Queequeg works his extraordinary effects by offsetting, literally and metaphorically, a realistic situation so overwhelming as to seem intolerable without his reassuring and numinous companionship.

The savage rituals and Ramadans prescribed by ancient myth and inscribed on the "living parchment" of Queequeg's own skin, provide for Ishmael a path of action, a symbolic action certainly, but one that allows the paralysis of conflict on the Pequod--a universe in microcosm--to give way to a new and radiant vision of illumination. In this context the very name Pequod is no accident. Ishmael made explicit reference to the consequences of the Pequot War:

> Pequod, you will remember, was the name of a celebrated tribe of Massachusetts Indians now extinct as the ancient Medes.[32]

Although Melville might be vague about the specific location of the Pequots, who were actually attacked by Puritans near Mystic,

Connecticut,[33] he is clear in defining a vengeful savagery that underlies white Christianity which the Indians themselves would be hard-pressed to emulate. Such a vision of white predators and Indian victims is mirrored in the more fundamental duality between the benign Queequeg and the destructive Ahab. For Ishmael, the refusal to consent to life's dissolution, to become "as much a savage as an Iroquois,"[34] becomes a means of establishing a metaphorical alliance with the life-giving forces of the Indian rather than the predatory instincts of the white man.

Such an alliance must be seen in relation to the whole action of Queequeg's and Ishmael's relationship in the novel, which moves toward deliverance from death not for the Indians but for a single white man. It is as if Queequeg's coffin-life buoy, graven with the hieroglyphic tattooing of his seemingly incomprehensible nature, is formed out of the very forces of man's deepest past which rise to sustain Ishmael from the sea that would drown him. For Ishmael, all is not as it was before Queequeg; the sacred-- the timeless world of the imagination--has for a time invaded the profane, and despite his sense of loss, a new vision is left to shape his mind and actions. He may recant, but he cannot forget.

This discussion of <u>Moby-Dick</u> has dealt exclusively with the metaphor of the Indian as it asserts one possibility of revelation in a soul or a society whose very needs appear to demand it. In Queequeg, a sense of human creative action is restored, and its imaginative, life-giving direction is momentarily clarified. Thus, it becomes increasingly possible for Ishmael to accept the necessary and tragic limitations in all possibilities. What Melville designs in his Indian metaphors may appear almost negligible when extracted from their living embodiment in the achieved vision of the entire work. But, for Melville, the Indian in his inherently metaphoric nature offers a whole spectrum of possibilities, of affirmative qualities that attach themselves to the tragic, and it is this which suggests how new and fundamental was his configuration, how far it removes Melville's Indian creation from the simple stereotypes of his contemporaries, James Fenimore Cooper, Richard Henry Dana and James Hall.

70

Thus, no formula can contain the open-ended, disparate metaphorical components of Melville's Indian, for he, like the white man, is perceived by Melville to be composed of contradictory elements, simultaneous and unresolved, and it is they which shaped his being.

Of all of Melville's contemporaries, only Nathaniel Hawthorne, in Melville's views, fully perceives the significance of Melville's concern with what he sees as the reality of living in a world of inconsistencies, of which the Indian is only one example. On 2 June 1851 Melville writes to Hawthorne from Arrowhead that "The Whale is only half way through the press." And then to describe his continuing encounter with the possibilities of the imagination he takes up an Indian metaphor of another kind altogether, he writes,

> For, in the boundless, trackless, but still glorious wild wilderness through which these outposts run, the Indians do sorely abound.[35]

In this "rather crazy letter in some respects," as Melville describes it, he also gives the "motto" for Moby-Dick, "(the secret one),--Ego non baptisto te in nomine--but make out the rest yourself,"[36] but it is the idea contained within the Indians' sore abundance in the realm of the imagination that is particularly significant here. In the metaphor the Indian becomes a kind of lightning rod for the projections of Melville --a symptom of a displaced "wild wilderness" of creativity, of a painful artistic impulse, and of an everpresent fear that its abundance may be destroyed. Thus, the image evokes a sensitive, yet powerful metaphor that draws a kind of magic circle around the Indian, drawing him within the vision of art Melville reveals whenever he turns in the Indian's direction.

In the light of the life-restoring imaginative abundance of the Indian metaphors Melville offers in Moby-Dick, the Indians in The Confidence-Man suggest the soreness of a darkened world in which growth has turned, like a cancer, into destruction. The Indian becomes a figure so alien and deformed as to embody malignity. The desire to hunt down this devil, to extirpate its threatening image, that is not so much of the Indian as of the white man's own self, leads to the inherent racism and genocide that is an implicit element of all those on the microcosmic world of the Fidéle.

A portrait of the grim reality of the American Indians' experience with the white man is initially presented in a parodic exploration of white charity, "The Widow and Orphan Asylum recently founded among the Seminoles."[37] A sense of Melville's basic compassion is conveyed as the reader is forced to ponder the need for such a charity. There is also an explanation and, to some extent, a justification, on the basis of the Indians' mistreatment by white pioneers, for the diabolical behavior of the red men. Shifting his ground as cunningly as the Confidence Man changes his mask, Melville then presents the white man's side of the story by making use of the popular fascination with Indian-shooting as a recognized American sport. Such "Injun fighters" as Tom Quick, Nick Stoner, and Colonel Moredock boast a long and successful history.

In his account of Colonel Moredock, Melville writes as if quoting James Hall's Sketches of History, Life, and Manners, in the West, but although the main facts of Moredock's life are retained, Melville freely rephrases Hall. For example, Hall attempts to give a history of white aggression on the frontier that took into account some of the feelings of the Indian:

> The whites were continually encroaching upon the aborigines, and the latter avenging their wrongs by violent and sudden hostilities. The philanthropist is surprised, however, that such feelings should prevail now, when these atrocious wars have ceased, and when no immediate cause of enmity remains; at least upon our side.[38]

Melville fails to follow Hall's narrative here, and instead presents a view of the Indian and indeed, of the backwoodsman as well, as wholly diabolical,

> Indian rapine having mostly ceased through regions where it once prevailed, the philanthropist is surprised that Indian-hating has not in like degree ceased with it. He wonders why the backwoodsman still regards the red man in much the same spirit that a jury does a murderer, or a trapper a wild cat--a creature, in whose behalf mercy were not wisdom: truce is vain; lie must be executed.[39]

For Melville's Moredock, a "pathfinder" and "captain in the vanguard of conquering civilization," sadly, no distinction is to be made between "panthers and Indians."[40] There is only one way for Moredock to make himself master of the discord of his own soul--by executing that which threatens it. Melville subtly intrudes and enlarges the scope of Hall's account with ironic asides that suggest that the white conquerors may yet be conquered by the Indians. Certainly Moredock's unquenchable passion for revenge becomes at least as diabolical as the Indians' cruelties. There is a sense in which the Indian Hater becomes his own nightmare version of his enemy. "But whether, on this or any point, the Indians should be permitted to testify for themselves, to the exclusion of other testimony, is a question for the Supreme Court.[41] Here the irony rests on Chief Justice John Marshall's decision against President Andrew Jackson's Indian Removal Policy which Jackson chose to ignore. Thus, even the Supreme Court may effect neither justice nor mercy where the Indians are concerned.

Moredock's violent creation "of what Indian-hating in its perfection is" appears just as lacking in genuine mercy and justice as the Cosmopolitan's idealized "love of the Indian." While the Cosmopolitan may get the last laugh when he refills his Indian calumet and asks, "Gentlemen, let us smoke to the memory of Colonel John Moredock,"[42] Melville's ironic thrust is clear: the man who is possessed by absolutes is more the prey of his own unconscious needs than he is the artculator of reality.

What Melville's confidence-man finally celebrates, in spite of himself, is the creative principle. The Indian metaphor here is the spiritual ideal of Queequeg imprisoned and rendered helpless. Full of admonitions, The Confidence-Man presents an inversion of human order into inhuman disorder. The ideal formulations of the white man become the frozen masks of a monstrous masquerade unrelated to the reality of his actions. In fact those actions themselves end by so destroying the very images which once conveyed order and compassion, that "the shooting at human beings... may be regarded as not wholly without the efficacy of devout sentiment."[43] Language itself seems no longer to signify in this metaphor of leagues of demons preying on a tribe that now includes all human beings. Yet in the creation of such metaphors Melville locates a means of containing and giving form to such disorder, by relating it to the larger order of his art, and thereby, provides an avenue of at least symbolic action against it. "Something further may follow of this masquerade."[44]

Whatever follows, there are, as always in Melville, no obvious conclusions or easy resolutions. By letting himself melt back into what remains primeval in his formalized society, Melville creates a varied portrait of the Indian whose composition invites and promises to repay all those who study it. It is an evocation which has stimulated the imagination of American artists over the past century, and a detached analysis of how this influence is felt necessarily tells us much about America's imaginative needs. Consciously or otherwise, Melville in some way perceives that the old set of Indian stereotypes would no longer serve those needs, perceives that just as the old ways of dealing with the Indian would fortunately die out, so would America's capacity to find surcease in simple fantasies of violence and nobility. It is hardly the destroying of these metaphors that Melville is after—metaphors are his gold—but rather a conscious awakening to the fact and function of metaphor in our lives, white and Indian, and a consequent sophistication that may keep us from the dangers of cultural self-deception and self-destruction.

NOTES

[1]The Letters of Herman Melville. Eds. Merrell R. Davis and William Gilman. (New Haven, 1960), p. 132.

[2]Hennig Cohen, Introduction, That Lonely Game: Melville, Mardi, and the Almanac. By Maxine Moore. (Columbia, Mo., 1975), p. xxv.

[3]Leon Howard, Herman Melville (Berkeley, 1951), pp. 34-37.

[4]The Literary World. IV (31 March 1849), 291.

[5]Literary World, IV, 293.

[6]Herman Melville, Moby-Dick. Eds. Harrison Hayford and Hershel Parker. (New York, 1967), ch. 72, 278-80.

[7]For further discussion of the Melville-Bradford relationship, consult Leon Howard, Herman Melville (Berkeley, 1967), pp. 17, 39.

[8]Alexander Bradford, American Antiquities and Researches into the Origins and History of the Red Race. (New York, 1843), pp. 415-16.

[9]Herman Melville, Typee: A Peep at Polynesian Life (Evanston and Chicago, 1968), p. 124.

[10]Melville, Typee, p. 201.

[11]Charles R. Anderson, Melville in the South Seas (New York, 1939), pp 191-93.

[12]Edwin Fussell, Frontier : American Literature and the American West (Princeton, N.J., 1965), pp. 236-37

[13]Melville, Typee, p. 237.

[14]Melville, Typee, p. 252.

[15]Herman Melville, White-Jacket (Evanston and Chicago, 1970), p. 187.

[16]Melville, White-Jacket, p. 151.

[17]Ibid., pp. 266-67.

[18]Anthony F.C. Wallace, "Revitalization Movements," American Anthropologist 58, no. 2 (April, 1966), 273.

[19]Eleanor Wilner, Gathering the Winds. (Baltimore, 1975), p. 26.

[20] Melville, Moby-Dick, ch. 1, p. 12.

[21] Ibid., ch. 10, p. 54.

[22] Ibid., ch. 10, p. 53.

[23] Ibid., ch. 110, p. 399.

[24] Ibid.

[25] Ibid., p. 395.

[26] Ibid., ch, 78, pp. 288-90.

[27] Robert Zoellner, The Salt-Sea Mastadon: A Reading of Moby-Dick (Berkeley, 1973), p. 231.

[28] Melville, Moby-Dick, ch. 110, p. 397.

[29] Ibid., ch. 110, p. 398.

[30] Ibid., ch. 78, pp. 289-90.

[31] Ibid., Epilogue, p. 470.

[32] Ibid., ch. 16, p. 67.

[33] For various sources on Melville's knowledge of the Pequots, see Kenneth Cameron's "Etymological Significance of Melville's Pequod," Emerson Society Quarterly. No. 29 (1962) and Robert Zoellner's The Salt-Sea Mastodon (Berkeley, 1973), pp. 67-68.

[34] Melville, Moby-Dick, ch. 57, p. 232.

[35] Davis and Gilan, eds. Letters, pp. 132-133,

[36] Ibid., p. 133.

[37] Herman Melville, The Confidence-Man. Ed. Hershal Parker. (New York, 1971), p. 24.

[38] James Hall, Sketches of History, Life, and Manners, in the West (Philadelphia, 1835), Vol. II, pp. 74-75, in The Confidence-Man. Ed. Hershel Parker (New York, 1971).

[39] Melville, Confidence-Man, p. 125.

[40] Ibid., pp. 126-27.

[41]Ibid., p. 127.

[42]Ibid., pp. 131-32.

[43]Ibid., p. 135.

[44]Ibid., p. 217.

CHAPTER FOUR:
MARK TWAIN AND THE INDIAN

> Would it not be prudent to get our Civilization-tools together, and see how much stock is left on hand in the way of Glass Beards and Theology, and Maxim Guns and Hymn Books, and Trade-Gin and Torches of Progress and Enlightenment (patent adjustable ones, good to fire villages with, upon occasion), and balance the books and arrive at the profit and loss, so that we may intelligently decide whether to continue the business or sell out the property and start a new Civilization Scheme on the proceeds?[1]

Mark Twain attacks "civilized" American society for many failures of mind and heart. Through the mask of Mark Twain Samuel Clemens projects a voice of "genial humorist, controlled ironist, savage satirist, avowed moralist" to force his readers to confront his own versions of aesthetic reality, versions that may be quite at variance with his readers' own.[2] Mark Twain's evaluation of nineteenth-century American illusions focuses with special care on those elements within the society which repress, exploit, and enslave through the romantization of ideas. The idea of the Indian provides a case for Mark Twain's analysis, one less abundantly penetrated than that of the Old South, but one that offers its own fascination metaphorical terrain. Mark Twain's imagination of the Indian, of the "Injun" as he refers to "Injun Joe" in The Adventures of Tom Sawyer, differs from that of Melville, Thoreau or Cooper. Yet like these literary artists, Mark Twain employs the figure of the Indian to make his own singular point of view clear, and like them, too, he is fundamentally evaluative of white Americans too content with easy images and comfortable "civility."

The historical context of Mark Twain's Indian metaphors marks a transition from the period of Melville, Hawthorne, Thoreau, and Cooper also. Before the Civil War Indian tribes within United States territory continued to offer armed resistance; they held the wilderness at least in the minds of whites until the period of the American Renaissance, c. 1850-1855. The United States government, Robert Berkhofer, Jr., notes, "essentially completed the conquest of the Indian by the end of the 1870's."[3] It is during the period of Mark Twain's literary career that all Native Americans come under the control of the United States government, and also during this period a range of self-professed humanitarian organizations develop specifically with the intention to reform, acculturate, and assimilate the entire native population. These reformers together with government officials believe that the "only hope of transforming the Indian lay in detribalizing him as a prelude to acculturation and assimilation. By 1890, these circumstances had produced what reformers and government officials of the day thought was the final solution to the Indian Problem allotment of reservation lands combined with American citizenship."[4] To absorb American Indian territory and exploit its riches and then to justify the action requires, as Helen Harris has observed, the indictment of the Indian.[5] But it also requires at least the illusion of reform so that humanitarian consciences might be placated. In Tom Sawyer Mark Twain scorns both the Indian and the reformers, and he satirizes the American literary portrayal of the Indian by suggesting that American writers must never have seen a canoe or set foot in the woods to commit such absurd hyperbole in their creations of Leatherstocking and all the rest. But Mark Twain goes further than merely exposing these failures in essays such as "Fenimore Cooper's Literary Offenses" (1895); he proposes in the Galaxy that the Indian "is a good, fair, desirable subject for extermination if ever there was one."[6] With Swiftian irony Mark Twain speaks the voice of white frontier America as it intrudes on the lands of the tribes and then demands U.S. Army protection and the extermination of the "Bloodthirsty Savages" it arouses. But the costs of total extermination come high. As a result of the pressures exerted by eastern reformers and of congressional concern over the expensiveness of Indian warfare, the reservation system evolves: "Not only was it considered more honorable but it was shown to be far cheaper to feed these nomadic buffalo hunters upon a reservation."[7] Mark Twain discovers in the Indian a being that will figure continuously in his symbolic vocabulary, just as that figure recurs in American experience. Although Mark Twain's Indian is not primarily a character-"Injun Joe" is only a "good, fair, desirable object for extermination" and not much of a real characterization--the Indian does figure as a metaphor and moral reference point.

The Indian's presence in Mark Twain's vision is both critical and reflective of the evolving desires and experiences of white America. Peace between Indians and whites in America comes less from the victories and defeats of the U.S. Army than from the destruction of the buffalo herds, death from poverty and disease, and the extension of American technological expertise through the Plains by the railroad.[8] The humanitarian sentiment of reformers, however genuine and well-meaning, proves just as destructive of Indian life as the economic forces which develop a transcontinental railroad. The power of white Americans becomes an overwhelming reality for the native population. The danger, violence, and destruction inherent in that reality is transformed in Roughing It (1872) into adventurous fun. In the book the narrator, "Mark Twain," begins by explaining that his tale is one in which he "may get hanged or scalped, and have ever such a fine time."[9] In the spirit of all this amusement, Mark Twain develops his contrast of Eastern and Western types, as the tenderfoot's eagerness for violence and riches evolves into the old-timer's experience and consciousness.[10] William Gibson observes that whatever Mark Twain "may have felt at the time in Nevada and California," he was writing Roughing It in Hartford, Connecticut, and "he could not accept the Western view unreservedly. Even before he left the West" he was not wholeheartedly approving "because he was recognizing its limitations."[11] The potential for a "fine time" in a territory renowned for its scalpings and hangings is ultimately less that satisfactory, except in the creation of a work of fiction dedicated to the remembrance of Westernness as metaphor.

That pleasurable vision of a "fine time" in <u>Roughing It</u> to be had in civilizing a continent is countered and developed metaphorically in The <u>Adventures of Tom Sawyer</u> (1876). Tom, who expresses an "ambition to be a discoverer," endures with his friend Huck a series of crises because of the Indian character, "Injun Joe." Distinctions between Injuns and whites are clear for the boys: "When you talked about notching ears and slitting noses I judged that that was your own embellishments, because white men don't take that sort of revenge. But an Injun. That's a different matter, altogether."[12] It is the ferocity of "Injun Joe" that is the cause of Tom and Huck and Becky's fear amid the darkness and danger of the McDougal cave, so much so that when "Injun Joe" dies Tom says he "felt an abounding sense of relief and security... he had not fully appreciated before how vast a weight of dread had been lying upon him since the day he lifted his voice against this bloody-minded outcast" at the trial of Muff Potter.[13] "Injun Joe" is exterminated accidentally, and Tom is said to feel a measure of relief because he has not been directly involved in the sealing up of the labyrinthian cave which is the Indian's natural habitat. Tom's moments in the cave come to suggest the pattern of white American ambitions to be "discoverers" with all the attendant violence and glory. In the cave Tom "might go down, and down, and still down, into the earth, and it was just the same-- labyrinth underneath labyrinth, and no end to any of these."[14] The American wilderness in all its seeming endlessness holds the treasure of "Injun Joe," who came into possession of it first and so he and the threat he holds must be removed before Tom may be triumphant. After days of fear and exploration within the cave, Tom believes he has found a "human hand" of assistance in the underworld wilderness. Tom raises a "glorious shout, and instantly that hand was followed by the body it belonged to--Injun Joe's."[15] Suddenly, the hand ceases to be "human" and becomes that of the "bloody-minded outcast," a being incapable of humanity who immediately flees following his contact with Tom and is hidden away in the cave forever. Tom escapes to tell his tale, for he is the narrator who presents the white man's side of the confrontation with the Indian, and then Tom returns again to the cave he "proposed to explore" with Huck and by and by he exclaims, "'My goodness, Huck, looky here!' It was the treasure box, sure enough."[16] The suppression of the Indian and the exploitation of his treasure provide the inevitable and happy conclusion to The Adventures of Tom Sawyer.

Mark Twain rejects any humanitarian sentiment concerning "Injun Joe" and supports the idea that white Americans may help themselves to Indian treasures of land and resources in the name of economic individualism, but in the sequel to The Adventures of Tom Sawyer, The Adventures of Huckleberry Finn (Tom Sawyer's Comrade), Mark Twain evaluates the paradoxes inherent in white American ideas of race. In Huck Finn he seeks to design a distinction between the so-called humanitarian values of the Sunday School and the human values of Huck and Jim. It is Jim, the black slave, who offers Huck a sermon on what it means to be a human being: "All you wuz thinkin 'bout wuz how you could make a fool uv old Jim wid a lie. Dat truck dah is trash; en trash is what people dat uts dirt on de head er dey fren's en makes 'em ashamed." Huck responds, "It made me feel so mean I could almost kissed his foot to get him to take it back. It was fifteen minutes before I would work myself up to go and humble myself to a nigger, but I done it, and I warn't ever sorry for it afterwards, neither."[17] Through the growing consciousness of Huck, Mark Twain evaluates the elements within nineteenth-century white American society which devise racial ideas that fail to perceive or take into account the humanity of Jim. Huck recognizes humanness in a "nigger" and acknowledges his own lack of human awareness. The vision of Mark Twain contains moral reference points vis-à-vis race which compel his readers to re-evaluate their own perceptions of human relations and their own capacity to create a "civilization," as Huck refers to it.

The failure of American society to understand both its strengths and its limitations provides the subject matter for Mark Twain's next major novel, A Connecticut Yankee In King Arthur's Court. Within the characterization of the Yankee, Hank Morgan, Mark Twain locates all the technological promise of American civilization: "Why," Hank declares, "I could make anything a body wanted anything in the world, it didn't make any difference what; and if there wasn't any quick new-fangled way to make a thing, I could invent one--and do it easy as rolling off a log."[18] As Henry Nash Smith has noted, the "comic contrast between medieval and modern manners rests on the assumption that the American common sense and commercial realism are axiomatically superior to the other-worldly ineptitude of the knights" or of any culture not that of enlightened industrial capitalism of the nineteenth-century.[19] At the center of the Yankee's narrative, Smith reminds us, is Mark Twain's vision of progress, a vision that contrasts a Utopian future of justice and enlightenment with the barbarism of ignorance and poverty of other societies. What is not technologically successful appears inevitably to be brutal and degrading. Or is it? Between Mark Twain's explicit endorsement of progress in the novel and his implicit revulsion over the potential menace within industrial systems, the artist devises a plot in which Morgan nearly destroys the civilized world he has sought to devise.[20] In the novel Mark Twain writes, "A man is a man, at bottom. Whole ages of abuse and oppression cannot crush the manhood out of him."[21] At the center of being is a humanity Mark Twain seeks despite all the ambiguities lie discovers within and without it.

Doubts concerning the meaning of civility are only one source of ambivalence for Mark Twain. Hamlin Hill observes that the artist was disturbed by doubts of his literary role also: "Was he a comedian or a moralist, or were the two roles identical? Was his proper vein the raucous Western tall tale or the genteel historical romance? These were questions he debated from the 1860's until the end of his life."[22] As Mark Twain perceives more and more imperialism in the glories of civilization, his ambivalence becomes clearly defined in his "strongest and most considered utterance on the subject of imperialistic war, 'To the Person Sitting in Darkness'" (1901).[23] The "person" referred to in the title of the piece is a figure to whom imperialistic societies bring the light of civilization and at the same time impose the consequences of "Progress and Enlightenment" Mark Twain writes,

The Head of every State and Sovereignty in Christendom, and ninety percent of every legislative body in Christendom, including our Congress and our fifty State legislatures, are members not only of the church, but also of the Blessings of Civilization Trust. This world-girdling accumulation of trained morals, high principles, and justice, cannot do an unright thing, an unfair thing, an ungenerous thing, an unclean thing. It knows what it is about.[24]

The irony is deadly; "civilized" governments know precisely what they are "about." They are about the economic and political exploitation of the weak, in Mark Twain's vision. By taking in everyone, but especially, the Person Sitting in Darkness, Progress and Civilization "can have a boom."[25]

The illusions inherent to the white American conceptions of progress and civility, more than specific ideas attached to the figure of the American Indian, are what challenge Mark Twain's imagination. If Mark Twain indicts destructive and ignorant "Injuns" as worthy of extermination, he also indicts white men who exploit victims of oppression for their own greed and false illusions of "civility." If Mark Twain explores the racial conscience of white Americans in Huck Finn, he supports the growing awareness of true human values in the nature of Huck himself. If Mark Twain examines with pride the technological accomplishments of civilization through the character of Hank Morgan, he questions their capacity to destroy not only the victims of technology but also its perpetrators. Mark Twain evaluates illusions which repress, exploit, enslave, and reform according to the desires of those in power. Mark Twain designs his own vision through his own images of a vernacular and growing consciousness of the humanness of man: "A man is a man, at bottom. Whole ages of abuse and oppression cannot crush the manhood out of him."

NOTES

[1] Mark Twain, To the Person Sitting in Darkness (New York, 1901). pp. 164-65.

[2] William Gibson, The Art of Mark Twain (New York, 1976), p. 29.

[3] Robert Berkhofer, Jr., The White Man's Indian (New York, 1978), pp. 166-76.

[4] Berkhofer, The White Man's Indian, p. 166.

[5] Helen Harris, "Mark Twain's Response to the Native American." American Literature, XLVI (January, 1975), 504.

[6] Contributions to the Galaxy 1868-1871 By Mark Twain, ed. Bruce R. McElderry, Jr. (Gainesville, Fla., 1961), p. 71.

[7] Berkhofer, The White Man's Indian, p. 167.

[8] Ibid.

[9] Mark Twain, Roughing It (Berkeley, 1972), p.43.

[10] Henry Nash Smith, "Mark Twain as Interpreter of the Far West: The Structure of Roughing It," The Frontier in Perspective (Madison, 1957), pp. 206-10.

[11] William Gibson, The Art of Mark Twain (New York, 1976), p. 47.

[12] Mark Twain, The Adventures of Tom Sawyer (Berkeley, 1982), p. 214.

[13] Ibid., p. 238.

[14] Ibid., p. 204.

[15] Ibid., p. 230.

[16] Ibid., p. 246.

[17] Mark Twain, The Adventures of Huckleberry Finn (New York, 1885), p. 121.

[18] The Works of Mark Twain, IX, 50

[19] Henry Nash Smith, Mark Twain's Fable of Progress (New Brunswick, N. J., 1964), pp. 75-84.

[20] James Hohnson, Mark Twain and the Limits of Power (Knoxville, Tenn., 1982), p. 154.

[21] The Works of Mark Twain, IX, 345.

[22]Hamlin Hill, <u>God's Fool</u> (New York, 1973), p. 271.

[23]Gibson, <u>The Art of Mark Twain</u>, pp. 149-57.

[24]Mark Twain, <u>To The Person Sitting in Darkness</u>, p. 175.

[25]Ibid., p. 176.

CHAPTER FIVE:
REFORMERS AND REDISCOVERERS:
TOWARDS A MODERN INDIAN VISION

It is a shame which the American nation ought not to lie
under, for the American people, as a people are not at heart
unjust. If there be one thing which they believe in more than
any other and mean that every man on this continent shall
have, it is 'fair play.' And as soon as they fairly understand
how cruelly it has been denied the Indian, they will rise up
and demand it for him. [1]

The distaste with which Mark Twain views the idea of imperialism is
shared by many of his contemporaries. Yet in the second half of the
nineteenth century the Indian in America comes to be regarded less as an
enemy and more as an example of arrested humanity, as a being who has
failed to raise himself as civilized men, because of their science, industry,
and Christianity have finally raised themselves. If "paternalism served the
nation rather well in the first half of the nineteenth century" by reducing
"Indians and Africans to the status of docile children in the minds of their
murderers and exploiters," as Carolyn Porter suggests, then the period
following the defeat of the Indian is marked by a humanitarian ideology of
such paternalism.[2] Mark Twain and his contemporaries are no more able
to withstand or change the forces of "civilization" than Thoreau or Melville.
Critics and literary artists of the latter half of the nineteenth-century offer a
challenging counter-current to an America intent on Manifest Destiny, but
like their predecessors, they devise metaphors of the American Indian
according to their own understanding of the Indian's problem rather than
as Native Americans understand the problem or themselves.[3] The
paradoxes inherent to white images of the Indian recur and evolve.

Helen Hunt Jackson examines federal Indian reports in her Century
of Dishonor (1881) and finds them "felled with eloquent statements of

wrongs done to the Indians, of perfidies on the part of the Government" in the maltreatment of the Delawares, Cheyenne, Nez Perces, Sioux, Poncas, and Cherokees.[4] She finds it startlingly simple to unearth a succession of broken treaties. Within a year of the publication of Century of Dishonor the Indian Rights Association was formed and by 1887 the Dawes Act, with its policy of allotment, is directed at breaking down the physical and legal separateness of Native Americans within the United States.

Vine Deloria, Jr., a Standing Rock Sioux and legal specialist in treaty policy, writes that the Dawes Act was misinterpreted by the Bureau of Indian Affairs as a means of exploiting the Indians."[5] Essentially the Dawes Act provides another case in point of the single constant in white Indian policy, including that of the most humanitarian intent,--white policy-makers know best for Indians in the end. The Dawes Act links citizenship to private land ownership in a compulsory manner without regard to the degree of acculturation or the nature of individual tribe's economic resources. In the process of allotment vast quantities of Indian land becomes white land. Robert Berkhofer writes that in the Act "reform and crass interests team up to perpetuate old results under a new guise."[6] As the tribes are forced to shred themselves and their land to meet the demands of United States policy, American literary artists respond. To reform the process of "reform" through the vision of Indian metaphor is these writers' concern.

In addition to publishing Century of Dishonor Helen Hunt Jackson was appointed a Commissioner of Indian Affairs by President Chester Arthur in July, 1883, and she uses the weight of her office to intervene and prevent illegal seizure of Indian land in California and to gather materials for a polemical novel, Ramona. This novel was a remarkable success, requiring three hundred printings, but it also serves to confirm many of the stereotypes and formulas which better and more critical writers of American Indian fiction seek to transcend. Mrs. Jackson's primary interest is to portray the decay of the patriarchical land system in Spanish California; Ramona herself exists within a sentimental vagueness of narrative structure and romantic caricature. As a version of the stereotyped American Indian princess--a nineteenth century Pocahontas--Ramona retains her Indian identity through her love of another Indian Alessandro, who provides her with an Indian name, Majel, and who protects her interests despite the intervention and oppression of the Spanish: "Remember, I am Ramona no longer," she insists at the conclusion of the novel.[7] Mrs. Jackson builds a case against the Spanish as a ruling class whose "religious devotion and race antagonism were so closely blended that it would have puzzled the subtlest of priests"; the avarice of the Spanish serves to render the Indians "helpless in the hands of great powers, (they) have all the ignominy and humiliation of defeat, and none of the dignities or compensations of the transactions" conducted for them.[8] Mrs. Jackson deliberately employs the Spanish as the source of all evil in Ramona as a means of distancing the source of white oppression as far as possible from protestant America, and she obviates individual tribal differences as a way of evolving an obscure and general "Indianness." Yet her didacticism is always clear and correct in its details: "The story of one tribe is the story of all, varied only by difference of time and place; but neither time nor place makes any difference in the main facts. Colorado is as greedy and unjust in 1880 as Georgia in 1830, and Ohio in 1795" when she is not writing fiction.[9] Mrs. Jackson died in 1885 without gaining any true reparation for the tribes. Her fictional Ramona achieves for her far more fame than the factual account of Century of Dishonor. If her facts are right, her vision of "the story of one tribe" being "the story of all" is not a valid one, for generalized notions of "Indianness" merely support stereotypical forms of racial prejudice. The real question of the "story" eludes us still.

Yet the power of the images of Ramona is retained and repeated in another vastly popular book, Laughing Boy which bears a real resemblance to Ramona in several other ways. Yet La Farge introduces the text by deliberately disclaiming any didactic purpose: "This story is meant neither to instruct nor to prove a point, but to amuse. It is not propaganda, nor an indictment of anything.[10] A Harvard trained

90

anthropologist with fieldwork experience in the Southwest, La Farge combines anthropological details concerning Native American religious ceremonies and artistic methods of weaving and silver-making with a narrative romance concerned like Ramona with the rediscovery of Indian identity through the love of a "blanket" Navaho named Laughing Boy. Slim Girl, the Indian woman who has received some education in white American schools for Indians, returns to Navaho territory and sees in Laughing Boy "a light with which to see her way back to her people."[11] Slim Girl is portrayed as the victim of white society and then the victimizer of Laughing Boy; she lies to him, manipulates him, cuckolds him with a white lover, and deliberately addicts him to alcohol. In the process of her destruction of Laughing Boy, she comes to represent elements in white society which destroy tribal life. Slim Girl is both destructive and admiring of Navaho ways of being, just as white society is ambivalent and paradoxical in its relation with Native American experience. The girl is killed by her finally rejected lover, and afterwards Laughing Boy discovers in his vision quest ceremony following her death "a deep sense of peace, and a rejoicing over ugliness defeated."[12] The triumph of the Native American is short-lived, as La Farge relates in the Foreword to the 1962 edition Laughing Boy:

> The beginning anthropologist who went among them could believe, as they did, that their general condition and mode of life, with all its hardships, simplicity, and riches, could continue indefinitely if only they were not interfered with. The collapse of that way of life began in 1933.[13]

The formulation of the Indian New Deal under Commissioner of Indian Affairs John Collier beginning in 1933 initiated policy changes aimed at the development of tribal economic bases and political autonomy. While "native autonomy and interests were better represented under the Indian New Deal than ever before in the history of United States policy--and perhaps subsequently as well," the intrusion of any federal policy creates inevitable change.[14] Change, an imposed and unyielding loss of past and concomitant loss of past identity, compels the "collapse" of old Indian modes of life. It is change and collapse which forms the center of Indian metaphor in the twentieth century.

White American writers come to see in the Indian an ideology of communal values that goes beyond the versions of identity crisis of Ramona and Slim Girl. Writers seek the values of community, spirituality, and reciprocity in the Indian in the twentieth century, just as their predecessors in the nineteenth century, Thoreau and Melville sought them. Whether those values exist in Native American culture or not does not matter--surely, those values exist to varying extents in every culture--what does matter is that the literary artists wish those values for themselves as an antidote to a materialistic and individualistic white America. While the actual qualities of Native American life vary, indeed still vary greatly, between Eastern woodland tribes, plains tribes, or the pueblos of the mesa to give only several of the most superficial examples, American authors, like Americans themselves, attribute the same characteristics and values to all. Government policy reflects this problem, so much so that for John Collier "all Indians became Pueblos in his vision, regardless of where or how they lived and regardless of Collier's belief that his program allowed for the multiplicity of tribal cultures and conditions.[15] From the first the Indian is a being created out of speculation or myth rather than reality, and this is the reason why Indian metaphors require such careful consideration, for when the Indian does not exist, he is invented. He is perceived to stand as the antithesis of culture and civilization, and therefore he possesses the capacity to reveal what his perceivers lost or repressed in becoming what they are.

In Willa Cather's The Professor's House such an indictment of American preoccupation with material possession is designed through a vision of a Pueblo village which becomes the purely beautiful pastoral center of the fiction. In this "world above the world" Cather creates characters who first discover, then fight over, and finally learn something from a cache of Indian treasure. Tom Outland finds the treasure and then has it stolen, but he grieves over its loss not for its monetary value: "I never thought of selling them, because they weren't mine to sell."[16] The other characters in the novel, aside from the sympathetic Professor St. Peter, are wholly caught up in a life of appearance and material possession and are devoid of fulfillment.[17] Yet Tom awakes on the mesa "with the feeling that I had found everything, instead of having lost everything," and he shares his vision with the Professor, who also comes to believe he had let something go and in the process becomes "outward bound" like Tom Outland.[18] In the process of relinquishing materiality--in the Professor's case he nearly dies by asphyxiation--Cather's characters come to discover a sense of meaning through their imagination of the Indian mode of life.

The possibility that "civilized" man might elude the demands and limitations of his materialism and individualism--even though that wealth and sense of personal identity are what provide the very conditions for his quest--and discover new ways to see and mean is a crucial element in the visions of Thoreau and Melville as well as in the American writers who follow them. By absorbing the regenerative force of native experience, the American literary comes to believe, men might achieve a mutual salvation. Even Mark Twain, who evaluates the native experience brutally, seeks such a salvation in such a mutuality. In the period following the American Renaissance, the defeat of the Indian and the entrenchment of whites marks the end of violent Indian hating--again Mark Twain provides a case in point, for even his notion of the Gosiute as "Goshoots" as a "sneaking, treacherous-looking race" becomes transmuted into the invention of a "person" lost in an imperialistic war of greed.[19] Although no longer offering any threat, Native American experience survives and thrives in white fiction. A hybridizing process occurs as white authors seek to "know and respect," as John Neihardt writes, "an ancient people with a rich culture that was dying out with the old, unreconstructed longhairs."[20] Neihardt's prose narrative Black Elk Speaks, a tale of the Sioux until their defeat at the Battle of Wounded Knee, as told by the Holy Man, Black Elk, offers a vision of the Indians' transcendent ability to see the otherness of things. It is this possibility of seeing through another eye which underlies not merely the vision of Neihardt, but also his contemporaries, Jack

London, Frank Waters and A. B. Guthrie. In <u>The Call of the Wild</u>, for example, London designs a journey by a young man, Buck, into the wilderness. There he seeks to be overwhelmed by his sense of a transcending euphoria:

> He was mastered by the sheer surging of life, the tidal wave of being, the perfect joy of each separate muscle, joint and sinew and that it was everything that was not death.[21]

To Buck's consciousness of his own mastery of nature and of himself there appears little ambiguity; the wild that is Buck's quarry is absorbed within the blood of the explorer of the new land. A. B. Guthrie examines the ambiguity felt by mountain men in his <u>The Way West</u> and <u>The Big Sky</u>. These men know the vitality of the wild and realize that by their very presence they will be its destruction:

> What was it in the past that pulled him back, that put the lines of wanting in his face sometimes when he didn't know that anyone was looking. Trapping? Indians? Buffalo? The wild and empty country? Evens himself could understand a love of them. He liked open land himself. But still a man must live ahead. Those times were gone.[22]

The achievement of America itself requires that "those times were gone;" however deeply they pull man back in search of the transforming strength those times engendered in the first place. For Frank Waters the historical contact between wild and western civilization signifies "one eternal theme--the inherent wholeness of man and his oneness with the entire universe."[23] In his <u>The Man Who Killed the Deer</u>, the quest for a reawakened awareness of the invisible creative powers of nature compel an exploration of Indian America, as he calls it. In their hybridizing process each of these authors employs the dreams they share with their readers: dreams of an untainted relation to nature and of a regenerative contact with Native Americans.

94

An Indian ideology offers a mythic dimension to the works of white writers here and also to the works of Faulkner and Hemingway which will be discussed in the following chapter, but the actual Native American experience in all its essential variance and cultural complexity is largely discounted even by the most sympathetic observers and designers of Indian metaphors. The visions of an angry Mark Twain, or a reforming Helen Hunt Jackson, of a detail-hungry Oliver La Farge, of a nearly despairing Willa Cather, of a respecting John Neihardt, of a euphoric Jack London, of a divided A. B. Guthrie, and of an insistently unifying Frank Waters reflect these literary artists' own society and own view of history in all of its paradoxes and ambivalences. It is a point of view that does not seek fully to comprehend the conflicts and contradictions inherent to the experience of Native Americans; it has enough difficulty coping with its own.

NOTES

[1]Helen Hunt Jackson, A Century of Dishonor (New York, 1881), p. 9.

[2]Carolyn Porter, Seeing and Being (Middletown, Conn., 1981), pp 233-35. Prof. Porter is concerned with the concept of reification as it influences the literature of Emerson, Henry James, Henry Adams, and William Faulkner.

[3]Robert Berkhofer, The White Man's Indian, pp. 192-93.

[4]Helen Hunt Jackson, Century of Dishonor, p. 338.

[5]Vine Deloria, Jr., Behind the Trail of Broken Treaties (New York, 1974), p. 6.

[6]Robert Berkhofer, The White Man's Indian, pp. 174-75.

[7]Helen Hunt Jackson, Ramona (New York, 1934), p 230.

[8]Ibid., pp 16-17.

[9]Helen Hunt Jackson, Century of Dishonor, pp. 337-38.

[10]Oliver La Farge, "Introductory Note to the Original Edition," Laughing Boy (New York, 1971). p. 9.

[11]Oliver La Farge, Laughing Boy, p. 45.

[12] Ibid., p. 11.

[13]"Foreword" p. 6.

[14]Robert Berkhofer, The White Man's Indian, pp. 176-86.

[15]Ibid., p. 185.

[16]Willa Cather, The Professor's House (New York, 1925), p. 242.

[17]David Stouck, Willa Cather's Imagination (Lincoln, 1975), pp 103-4.

[18]Cather, The Professor's House, p. 282.

[19]Mark Twain, Roughing It (Hartford, 1872), p. 146.

[20]John Neihardt, Patterns and Coincidences (Columbia, Mo., 1978) p. 36.

[21] Jack London, The Call of the Wild (New York, 1963), p. 49.

[22] A. B. Guthrie, The Big Sky (New York, 1947), p. 338.

[23] Frank Waters, "Foreword," Mountain Dialogues (Athens, Ohio, 1981), p. ix.

CHAPTER SIX:
MODERN VISIONS: HEMINGWAY AND FAULKNER

We have taken from the defeated
What they had to leave us--a symbol:
A symbol perfected in death.

T.S. Eliot, "Little Gidding, III."[1]

I seek an image of the modern mind's discovery of itself.
William Butler Yeats, The Words Upon the Window
Pane.[2]

The Indian, as earlier imagined by Herman Melville and Henry David Thoreau, speaks to the modern mind in its discovery of itself. A symbolic matrix in which artists of different times discover different meanings, the Indian metaphor becomes entangled with modern man's quest not so much for bears and Indians but for his innermost self. Even more important for the American literary artists to be examined here, Ernest Hemingway and William Faulkner, is the quest to nourish and enrich that self in the natural order.

The best arrowheads went all to pieces.
Ernest Hemingway, "Now I Lay Me."[3]

Ernest Hemingway's Indian plays a role in the collected first forty-five stories written during the years 1923-1933. There the Indian performs a symbolic or even ritualistic function in the service of the artist and the service of the white man, Nicholas Adams. The recurrent character in the stories, Nick, is not Hemingway himself, but the Ojibways in the tales are an Indian tribe Hemingway knew, and they appear in the ten stories which record Nick's growing up. The Ojibways Hemingway creates are seen as abstractions of Indian character far more than as realistic portraits of actual Indians.

For Hemingway the antitheses, and yet ironic proximity, between images of love and life and pain and death are central to the creation of this art. Such antitheses are, of course, far more fully developed in symbolic terms in the longer fictions, The Sun Also Rises (1926) and A Farewell to Arms (1929). But it is in these early stories that Nick takes up the role that Jake Barnes and Frederick Henry will later assume--that of detached observer viewing a world that left him at once amused and sick at heart.[4]

In the divided vision of the tales, the Indians command a remarkable range of sensual and imaginative resources, but at the same time they are made to embody a heartland of darkness and death. In "Ten Indians" the young Nick tells of feeling "hollow and happy inside himself" after his adolescent sexual initiation with a girl, Prudence Mitchell, but during a ride in a neighbor's wagon back from town past nine drunken Indians he is disillusioned. His girl, the tenth Indian, appears to have been seen "thrashing around" with someone else. The focus is, as always in the tales, on Nick's inner response: "If I feel this way," Nick tells himself, "my heart must be broken." Under the surface we perceive an intensity of passion as well as an awakening of his own imperturbability: in the morning "he was awake a long time before he remembered that his heart was broken."[5] His nostalgic reminiscence of Prudie, later transmuted into Trudy, shows the Indian as truly present only in recollection. The Indian exists in the mind only, in a world, he is almost relieved to note, now perhaps clear of entangling alliances with the potentiality to hurt.

Later in "Fathers and Sons" Nick recalls Prudie, or Trudy, as she is now named, as the one who "did first what no one has ever done better,"[6] but the real center of his recollection is in his concern not merely in the confusion, pleasure, and pain inherent to human sexuality, but in the problem of generation itself. As the mind of Nick moves from his father to his son, the relationships between the generations appear interpenetrated into two opposing and irreconcilable choices: the world of love and perpetuity is set off against that of fear and entanglement. Between these two sets of emotions, Nick is unable or, indeed, unwilling to choose. Nick has loved his father "very much and for a long time," and the father loves his son, but,

> Now, knowing how it had all been, even remembering the earliest times before things had gone badly was not good remembering. If he wrote it he could get rid of it.[7]

There is much more to "Fathers and Sons" than an act of personal exorcism however difficult. By talking about his father to his young son, Nick appears to rid himself of the oppressions of his past, of fatherly advice that is "unsound on sex"[8] and of his father's too early death at his own hand.

Hemingway, Carlos Baker has observed, means to shunt off the old wars between generations, between individuals, between nations, by writing them out, getting rid of them by setting the conflicts down in all the true and interwoven strands of honor and horror.[9] To destroy by the means Nick describes--"if he wrote it he could get rid of it"--is also to create by embodying the record of his suffering in the permanent, transcending form of art. Hemingway's Indians are an aspect, a symbol, within the structure of his art.

We may wonder why Hemingway nowhere appears to commit himself against the oppression of the Indian, or to become their defender, but the answer is simply that his Indians are truly present only as ideas or symbols of his imagination, only as figures inextricably linked within the conceptions of his own past. Thus, his Indians in the story, "Indian Camp," seem to tell us more about Ernest Hemingway than about Ojibway braves. In the tale Nick appears again as a detached observer of a scene of horror that involves his father, once again, and, again, the Indians. His physician

100

father is asked to assist an Indian woman, who had been in labor for two days. As she undergoes a caesarian with no anesthetic, a jackknife for a scalpel, and fishing line for surgical thread, the father of her child slashes his throat. His suicide appears inconsistent with Indian courage and stoicism; but in Hemingway's vision self-destruction in the face of the pain of childbearing appears a means of escape when every way of love and life seems blocked and threatening. Life itself seems a war-like test of survival. The young Indian mother, unlike Catherine Barkley in A Farewell to Arms, is able to endure the bearing of a child. But her husband is dead, and all the survivors, including Nick and his father, are permanently scarred by the experience. The future is uncertain--except that they are sure that they, too, will die in the end.

That the Indian may be a guide through the terrors of death, a figure who "took it all pretty quietly,"[10] as we are told of the suicidal Indian in Indian camp, is reflected in what Nick told of the Indians and his father in "Now I Lay Me." In this story, which begins with Nick's insomniacal ramblings as a war casualty, the artifacts of the Indian are made to show a symbolic function in the service of the artist. Here, too, Indians are connected to the image of Nick's father. The emphasis here, as in another river story, "Big Two-Hearted River," is an inner experience. Nick searches for a command of self and of imaginative resources in a metaphorical "fishing" in "made-up streams." He feels under the surface of consciousness a nostalgic remembrance of things of the past and an intense reawakening of passionate emotions:

> It was like being awake and dreaming. Some of those streams I still remember and think I have fished in them, and they are confused with streams I really know.[11]

Amid his sense of dissolution comes a vision of discovery of the creative imagination allied to an experience in his childhood But, then, another image, this time of destruction, but still naturally connected to his memories of fishing in Indian streams, intrudes on his consciousnes,

> I remember how my mother was always cleaning things out
> and making a good clearance. One time when my father was
> on a hunting trip she made a good thorough cleaning out of
> the basement and burned everything that should not have
> been there.[12]

The things that should not have been there include his father's prize Indian relics, "stone axes and stone skinning knives and tools for making arrowheads and pieces of pottery and many arrowheads"[13] Later, as he rakes over the ashes, Nick recalls that his father "spread all the blackened, chipped stone implements on the Paper and then wrapped them up. 'The best arrow head went all to pieces,' he said."[14] Nick's ruminations lead him ritualistically to hunt through the shadows of death and suffering for a kind of survival. The black and chipped Indian relics are burned in a fire that reaches all men eventually. The Indian has become in the blackened bits and pieces of death a means of conveying Nick's own black and broken self, helpless and vulnerable, unable even to comfort or console his own much-loved father. The death of the Indian brave in "Fathers and Sons" and the burning of the arrowheads in "Now I Lay Me," exactly completes the symbolic structure of Hemingway's Indians, who begin as sexual beings with natural resources beyond civilization's threat. But then this image of life and love, Nick comes to discover, is lost--first in disillusion, then in horror, finally in the burning of the only things that still remain of the Indian, his arrowheads.

In Hemingway's vision, the symbols of life and love are opposed to death and war; the world of Jake Barnes and Pedro Romero is set off against that of Robert Cohn and Brett Ashley in The Sun Also Rises just as the image of safety and "separate peace" in the mountains of A Farewell to Arms is contrasted with horror and war on the plain. It is possible to perceive a way in which the Indian virtues of stoicism, sensuality, machismo, and brotherhood conform to, even constitute the lineaments of the Hemingway hero. These virtues become transferred, or perceived in Hemingway's imagination, in the Indian characters he encounters up in

102

Michigan and are qualities Hemingway found in the Ojibway and then wrote into his other male characters. For Hemingway, rough and friendly camaraderie the informal brotherhood that exists between men through bylaws which are not written down or directly articulated but nonetheless are perfectly understood and rigidly adhered to by the contrasting parties is a significant association. It ceases to matter whether one's male companion is Indian or white, African or Italian, what is meaningful is that wholly happy and normal condition which men, fishing or drinking or talking together, can build into a world of their very own. This is the world in the Burgeate of Jake Barnes and Bill Gorton, in the Gorizia of Lieutenant Henry and Doctor Rinaldi, and in the Guardarrama hide-out of Robert Jordan and Anselmo.[15] The phase of masculine life may, indeed, must be challenged by another phase of life with women so that a state of tension is set up between the two, and, in each case, when a choice is compelled, the masculine figure accepts his painful and inextricable connections with family and home and children, as in the story "Now I Lay Me." Domestic responsibility represents a powerful notion, even attraction, but it could conceivably destroy all those things symbolized by the good companionship of trusted men, fathers and sons all.

In his Indian figures, Hemingway designs a pattern of art which includes the Indian. His is an Indian whose metaphorical function is chiefly defined by and meant to show his service to the artist. It is a ghostly service, submerged and haunting, a "blackened and chipped" memorial to all that has gone and seems without hope of recovery.

Sam Fathers set me free.
William Faulkner, Go Down, Moses.[16]

William Faulkner creates Indian metaphors that reveal a deep, almost religious sense of the permanence and richness of the American landscape as well as the idea of the American preoccupation with the problem of land ownership. In the face of a gradually diminishing pastoral

America, Faulkner's white men invade an inward terrain, with Indians as their guides; they seek to use the red man's primal power and life-restoring imagination for their own salvation.

In a number of stories, from "Red Leaves" (1930) onward, Faulkner demonstrates his fascination with the wilderness and with the narrative and symbolic potentialities of the Indian. It is in the short fictions, later gathered together in the Collected Stories under the heading, "The Wilderness," and in Go Down, Moses that Faulkner recreates the past of Yoknapatawpha, a land possessed by its own history at the same time that it seeks to destroy the history of the Indian.

"The ghost of that ravishment lingers in the land," Faulkner writes while lecturing at the University of Virginia in 1957, for "the land is inimical to the white man." And the dispossession of the Indian, in Faulkner's vision, is mirrored in the degradation of slavery and in the South's defeat in the Civil War. The word Yoknapatawpha is taken from the Chickasaw name for the Yocona River, which Faulkner translates as "water flowing slow through the flatland."[17]

This discussion of the Indian metaphor in "The Wilderness" and Go Down, Moses deals not so much with how "a man of another race becomes an Indian"[18] but instead with the metaphor of the Indian as it asserts one possibility of illumination in a darkened world whose needs appear to demand it.

The theme of the wisdom to be derived from the Indian and his wilderness is, for Faulkner, a deeply complex one which must always be juxtaposed against the theme of the injustice to blacks. To learn the meaning of the Indian's mythic wilderness is to perceive not merely human struggles for power and control but also the abuse and destruction of the natural order of the American landscape. Lewis Dabney writes in the conclusion to his study,

Whatever the source of the national belief in the Vanishing American's return, Faulkner held to and reinforced it in the eclipse of the southern tribes. The literary man's material was the moralist's alternative to the plantation and to mechanized modernity. Blacks and whites purified by the Indian culture and meeting on this ground-this is Faulkner's romantic melting pot mythology.[19]

I would suggest that Faulkner's sources for the return of the Indian's revealing spiritual presence are to be found in his reading of James Fenimore Cooper and Herman Melville,[20] in his mystical realization of nature--a theme which runs through American literature from Henry David Thoreau and Walt Whitman to Robert Frost,[21]--and in his own "compassion," as he put it, "for the anguish that the wilderness itself may have felt."[22] These are more than the resources of a romantic melting pot mythology. They are something quite different. The inner world that Faulkner explores becomes revalued. The still essentially hidden crises of soul and society which Melville and Thoreau illuminated so powerfully in their century, provide Faulkner with the means to see in the Indian a defense of inner life, of imagination itself. His revelation of the power of aesthetic vision helps to illuminate the despair of his contemporaries, Indian and white, who have increasingly looked to Faulkner for a prophet voice that may clarify their growing sense of desperation even if it could not be resolved.

Faulkner, then, provides a visionary grammar of the Indian in the twentieth century, offering, like Melville and Thoreau, both compassion and insight, and like them shedding light on the powerful but darkened imaginations of twentieth-century Indians themselves. The young Faulkner is fascinated with the telling of hunting tales and with the lore of the Indian. His knowledge of both is based on firsthand experience, as his brother John recalled in his "affectionate reminiscence," far more than on anthropological knowledge. As his conception of the Yoknapatawpha chronicles develops Faulkner remains rather unconcerned about historical accuracy or even about tribal origins. Thus, in "A Justice," written in 1931, the Indian Doom is called a Choctaw, but in later tales he is Chickasaw. Elmo Howell observes that Faulkner appears quite "unconcerned about variation in customs and ceremonies,"[23] but in fact Faulkner quite deliberately blends and transforms the lore of the Indian to meet his artistic purpose. Faulkner himself serves an apprenticeship in the woods, "killed his buck and was blooded, and he also killed a bear.[24] Faulkner writes that the wilderness is alive with

> the myriad life which printed the dark mold of these secret and sunless places with delicate fairy tracks, which, breathing and biding and immobile, watched him from beyond every twig and leaf until he moved, moving again, walking on...[25]

Something of the abundance and freedom of the Indian's wilderness provides Faulkner with a conception of nature that amounts to the sacramental.[26] His vision of the Indian evolves slowly, and within it Faulkner achieves to some degree the fusion of a number of apparently disparate ideas, rooted in personal experience if not accurate anthropology, which nonetheless long occupy his imagination.

Faulkner's metaphor of the reunion of suffering man, whether white or black or Indian, with his wandering soul emerges in the story "Red Leaves." There the spiritual antecedents of Sam Fathers live out the origins of the guilt of the McCaslins. Old Carothers McCaslin bought land from the money-hungry Indian chief, who himself possessed it by treachery and who introduced slave-holding into the tribal system. Here there is no sentimentalizing; both the Indian and the white man share in the act of corruption.[27] The chief, using the profits from his land deals and slave trade, journeys to Paris and returns with a pair of red slippers. His son kills the chief in order to possess the slippers for himself and then engages in the pursuit and ritual killing of a slave, who will be buried with the dead chief. At the end of the chase the slave looked back and up at them through the cracked mud mask. His eyes were bloodshot, his lips cracked upon his square short teeth.. He watched them quietly until one touched his arm. "Come," the Indian said, "You ran well. Do not be ashamed."[28]

It is as if the pursuing of the slave has become for the lost and degraded tribe a means of partial restoration in the face of defeat by the whites and, indeed, by their own now dead chief, the members of the tribe seek a rite of renewal and a way of purification. The dismemberment and descent of the slave, who has been bitten on the arm by a serpent, a creature of the Indians' world of spirits, becomes a reminder to the Indians that there is a realm of spirit, which discloses itself in rites and visions, and which somehow holds the key to renewed harmony within the tribe. The dead chief and his son have betrayed all human values and even turned their power against their own tribe. The slave becomes a lightning rod for the negative projections of the Indians--a symptom of displaced self-hatred and of repressed impulses--as well as a source of tribal restoration. When to assume guilt for their own misfortunes is unbearable or seems unforgivable, men, to escape their pain, project it onto those figures who are alien or deformed enough to seem to embody malignity.[29] But belief in such rites, however momentarily valuable, provides for only the expression of symptom, never a cure. It leaves, as Faulkner suggests here, the essential cause of the social malaise quite untouched.

In the other tales of "The Wilderness" and, particularly, in Go Down, Moses Faulkner explores the causes of the sickness of the soul he uncovers in "Red Leaves." Seeing the metaphor of the Indian as a way of containing and giving form to internal and white disorder, Faulkner relates the Indian to a larger order of which he is but a part, and perceives in the Indian's relation to the civilized world, a microcosm reflective of the malaise of slavery and injustice.

In the stories, "The Wilderness," "Lot," "A Justice," and "A Courtship," Faulkner examines Yoknapatawpha's Chickasaws in a comic mode. Here the treatment of the theme of the Indian, while often lighthearted, contains a power to convince us of the existence of a tribal world not merely prior to slavery but prior to civilization. Faulkner's Indians also possess the power to purify, to work as a counter-current to the civilized order when they confront it. For example, in "Lot" the Indians exist in the realm of fantasy where there is no injustice. They sell their land, then get rid of the buyer and retrieve it all, but all the while they tell each other, "We'll have to try to act like these people believe that Indians ought to act."30

Faulkner, who throughout his lifetime observes the influence of Herman Melville on his fiction, here employs a conceit that Melville, among others, borrows from Montaigne's "Of Cannibals." The notion that cannibals are more Christian than Christians, or Indians more shrewdly civilized than whites, is based on the deflation of racial stereotypes. Here Faulkner forces on his reader a reawakening of an image of the Indians as wholly human, and further, there is a sense in which the reader's own racism may be exposed.

Such exposure, though in the realm of fantasy, is one of the Indian's power to purify, to work his restorative insight within the world of civilization, and yet in the process be dispossessed or dispossess himself of his greatest resource, the wilderness itself. In "A Courtship" Faulkner designs an Indian-white romance between an Indian, Ikkemotubbe, and a white steamboat pilot, David Hogganbeck, who is the grandfather of the hunter Boon Hoggenbeck. Here the white man and the Indian are presumably vying for the hand of an Indian girl, Log-in-the-Creek, but in their pursuit of heroic struggles and epic contests the two men scarcely notice the infinitely desirable Log-in-the-Creek. In fact, their relationship mirrors that of Queequeg and Ishmael on the Pequod and Huck and Jim on the raft, far more than it does the conventional relation of rivals over love. Both David and Ikkemotubbe fail to win Log-in-the-Creek, perhaps because they barely pay attention to her, but they find true reconciliation in an alliance of their own. But finally here, too, as on the raft of the Pequod, the possibilities of brotherhood are ultimately destroyed by the civilized evils of slavery and injustice.

In "A Justice" Ikkemotubbe acquires a steamboat of his own as well as a group of his own slaves and, thereby, destroys the simple economy of his tribe. Faulkner's Gothic plot, which includes the sending of a naked Indian to Paris and the setting up of a sachem as an entrepreneur in another version of Life on the Mississippi, appears less concerned with the Indians than with the symbolic possibilities they present. For having himself set into motion the dispossession of the wilderness, Faulkner's Indian chief, now symbolically named Doom--in a kind of projection of Faulkner's doom-laden vision--affects the transformation of the tribal hunting grounds into a private game preserve for men like the McCaslins. The abuse and destruction of the wilderness, so beautiful in its natural and original state, may never be restored. The hunt for a "true wilderness" which occurs in Go Down, Moses provides the means of symbolic action. The genius of the imagination re-imagines a world with the communal values of the Indian at least momentarily restored.

The quest of Go Down, Moses has obvious parallels to the mythic journeys of Ishmael and Queequeg in Moby-Dick and to Thoreau's questors in A Week on the Concord and Merrimack Rivers, Walden and The Maine Woods. In Faulkner's vision, the hunt is undertaken by a young man, Isaac McCaslin, who, like his brother pursuer of a redeemed and hard-won manhood, is accompanied by a black-Indian guide, Sam Fathers. Sam is both the master of the hunting ritual and the caretaker of his Chickasaw totem animals. But more even than these roles Sam acts as Ike's guide to the world of the spirits, a realm of abundance, equivalence, and amity. This world whose "edges," Faulkner tells us, "were being constantly and punily gnawed at by men with ploys and axes who feared it,"[31] is almost hallucinatory in its power to convince us of the existence of a wilderness of no sin, no evil, no injustice.

Here the relationship between Ike and Sam Fathers appears not simply in the form of a boy and a dying Indian; nor are they merely representatives of differing races--foils to one another. Instead we perceive them as two individuals struggling through this time of destruction which engages them as

> men, not white nor black nor red but men, hunters with the will and hardihood to endure and the humility and skill to survive, and the dogs and the bear and deer juxtaposed and reliefed against it, ordered and compelled by and within the wilderness in the ancient and unremitting contest.[32]

Ike's skill as a woodsman is derived from Sam Father's, and is used in what was once the Indians' own terrain. Ike's repudiation of his white inheritance is inextricably linked to this fact, and is itself at least symbolic means of making amends:

> Sam Fathers said, 'Now. Shoot quick and shoot slow' and the gun leveled rapidly without haste and crashed and he walked to the buck lying still intact and still in the shape of that magnificent speed and bled it with Sam's knife and Sam dipped his hands into the hot blood and marked his face forever while he stood trying not to tremble, humbly and with pride too though the boy of twelve had been unable to phrase it then: I slew you; my bearing must not shame your quitting life. My conduct forever onward must become your death; marking him for that and for more than that: that day and himself and McCaslin juxtaposed not against the tamed land, and the old wrong and shame itself, in repudiation and denial at least of the land and the wrong and shame even if he could cure the wrong and eradicate the shame.[33]

Such a vision requires of Ike, who still is unable "to phrase it" for himself, an action, which if it cannot materially modify the injustice wrought by civilization, it at least acknowledges the need for expiation. "Many-fathered" by Buck whom he has never known, by his cousin Cass, by Sam Fathers, and by the wilderness itself, Ike attempts to expiate the sin "against the tamed land" committed by his grandfather and by the corrupted Indian, Ikkemotubbe. But these individuals are, of course, not the only ones to blame. It is the condition of extremity and crisis--of oppression, disorder, and disharmony--which the civilized order has imposed on what was once the wilderness, unfallen and unexploited, that is to blame. Ike's experience in that still untamed wilderness, with the Indian Sam Fathers as a guide, produces in him a vision derived out of the deep social crises of his time; it is the product of an individual imagination that shares fully in a collective experience of injustice and disorder. It is in such a visionary as Sam that Faulkner the artist sees a transformative and regenerative power both for the individual in which the vision has occurred and for the collectivities in which the vision may find communal resonance and assent.

Ike's journey to visionary experience involved an imaginative return to the past--a return via a primal rite that renews his perception of the spirit of the wilderness. Having "marked his face forever" Sam has touched Ike with his Indian guardian spirit hands and given him a power that marks his adolescence, a power which draws all forms together into a single form and which contains within it a basic assurance of life's primacy in what seems otherwise merely a degrading cycle of life and death. After serving his apprenticeship in this alien world, Sam's "true wilderness," Ike returns. But unlike Ishmael in Moby-Dick Ike is unable to tell the tale. His experience in the other world of the Indian and of imagination, while first hand, becomes mixed and muted by the misunderstandings and confusions of his family, his failed marriage, and especially of his lost son, the child to whom Ike wishes most to tell his tale.

If Ike can not tell it, if he is only a temporary guest," and Sam Fathers, now dead, is the "mouthpiece of the host,"[34] then it is required of Faulkner, as artist, to bear witness to the necessity for and impossibility of human continuity through vision. The artist's concern for perpetuity, for an object that "could continue to live past the boy's seventy years and then eighty years, long after the man himself had entered the earth as chiefs and kings enter it,"[35] is Faulkner's insistent effort. It is an effort that contains far more than a conception of the Particular inhuman forms of civilization which enslave human beings and destroy the wild land and its people Faulkner seeks no less than the reawakening of a vision of an ideal world. Thus, in the mind of Ike,

> it seemed to him that at the age often he was witnessing his own birth. It was not even strange to him. He had experienced it all before, and not merely in dreams.[36]

In such a metaphor of rebirth, which the present order of the land and its people betrays, a moment of reawakening is recaptured. No longer does man's history appear as merely the monotonous repetition of mindless actions and cycles of life and death, no more is man simply a small appendage in a process he can not comprehend: "Sam Fathers set me free."[37] Faulkner attempts to restructure the world of Ike in the wilderness with images of the mythological numinous and of compensatory freedom. It is not a gratuitous delusion, but a moving evocation, rich in its power to convince us of the existence of a wilderness world devoid of injustice and oppression. Under the tutelage of the wilderness and its human representative, Sam Fathers, Ike gathers a knowledge of the bear within. For it is the inner realm, rather than the external one, that contains within it the full meaning of liberation,

> He had not stopped, he had only caused quitting the knoll which was no abode of the dead because there was no death, not Lion and not Sam: not held fast in earth but free in

earth and not in earth but of earth, myriad yet undiffused of every myriad part.[38]

Like Faulkner, Melville earlier explored the symbolic significances of the Indian deep "in the heart of that almighty forlornness"[39] of destruction and death, where the primal past appears to break through from the vortex, like Queequeg's coffin, and rises to restore the living. Once a sense of human creative action and possibility is restored, it becomes increasingly possible for the individual to understand a means of reparation that goes far beyond Ike's somewhat puny and even inconsistent acts of repudiation.

The imaginative world contains a sure assertion, perhaps the only possible affirmation against decomposition in the work of art. But that world also contains admonitions. For once again the imagination of the Indian set limits to its own vision: Queequeg's coffin is empty, Ishmael remains an orphan; Sam Father is dead, Ike is utterly alone. Ishmael and Ike are survivors, not saviors. That their common survival is discovered in the forces of man's deepest past with an Indian who represents those forces as their companion and guide, draws them together in a metaphorical celebration of the aesthetic power generated by the image of the Indian itself. It is as if the very presence of the Indian constitutes proof that precisely those civilized institutions that most threaten the freedom of the individual may be transcended, if only momentarily, by the individual imagination. With that perception we may come gradually to see that the Indian, and those who dream along with him, may perhaps be said to have won the battle after all.

NOTES

[1] T.S. Eliot, "Little Gidding, III," Collected Poems 1909-1962 (New York, 1963), p. 203.

[2] William Butler Yeats, The Words Upon the Window Pane (Dublin, 1934), p. 3.

[3] Ernest Hemingway, The Short Stories (New York, 1953), p. 366.

[4] Carlos Baker, Hemingway: The Writer as Artist (Princeton, 1963), p.77.

[5] Hemingway, The Short Stories, p. 336.

[6] Ibid., p. 497.

[7] Ibid., p. 491.

[8] Ibid., p. 490.

[9] Baker, Hemingway, p. 77.

[10] Hemingway, The Short Stories, p. 94.

[11] Ibid., p. 364.

[12] Ibid., pp. 365-66.

[13] Ibid., p. 366.

[14] Ibid.

[15] Baker, Hemingway, pp. 120-21, 132-33.

[16] William Faulkner, Go Down, Moses (New York, 1942), p. 300.

[17] Frederick Gwynn and Joseph Blotner, eds., Faulkner in the University (Charlottesville, Va., 1959), pp. 43, 74.

[18] Lewis Dabney, The Indians of Yoknapatawpha (Baton Rouge, La., 1974), p. 154.

[19] Ibid., p. 154.

[20] Joseph Blotner, Faulkner: A Biography (New York, 1974), pp. 68, 101, 715, 1045, 1054, 1109, 1213.

[21] Daniel Hoffman, "William Faulkner: 'The Bear' "Landmarks of American Writing. Ed. Hennig Cohen. (New York, 1969), p. 243.

[22] Gwynn and Blotner, eds. Faulkner in the University, p. 277.

[23]Elmo Howell, "William Faulkner and the Chickasaw Funeral," American Literature, XXXVI (January, 1965), 523-25.

[24]John Faulkner, My Brother Bill (New York, 1963), p. 158.

[25]Faulkner, Go Down Moses, p. 328.

[26]Cleanth Brooks, William Faulkner: The Yoknapatawpha Country (New Haven, 1963), pp. 261- 68, 269.

[27]Ursula Brumm, "Wilderness and Civilization: A Note on William Faulkner," Partisan Review, XXII: 3 (Summer, 1955), 340-50.

[28]William Faulkner, "Red Leaves," Collected Stories (New York, 1950), p. 330.

[29]Eleanor Wilner, Gathering the Winds (Baltimore, 1975), pp. 68-70.

[30]Faulkner, "Lo!," Collected Stories, p. 401.

[31]Faulkner, Go Down, Moses, p. 193.

[32]Ibid., pp. 191-92.

[33]Ibid., p. 351.

[34]Ibid., p. 171.

[35]Ibid., p. 155.

[36]Ibid., pp. 195-96.

[37]Ibid., p. 300.

[38]Ibid., p. 328.

[39]Herman Melville, Moby-Dick. Eds. Harrison Hayford and Hershel Parker. (New York, 1967), p. 301.

CONCLUSION

> There, then, he sat, the sign and symbol of a man without
> faith, hopelessly holding up hope in the midst of despair.
> Herman Melville, Moby-Dick.[1]

No simple conclusions or easy resolutions mark the broad literary
phenomenon of the Indian in American literature. The imagination of the
Indian has become a guide here to the workings of the American
imagination at large, because it embodies the expression of man creating a
civilized order while being influenced by that which he seeks to civilize. In
that aesthetic process he rediscovers the collective nature of an individual
humanity that transcends racial distinctions even as it marks them. The
metaphorical Indian represents, above all, a will to connection. In visions
that reveal the hopeless holding of hope, as Melville designs one, men out
of their own despair seek a transformative sustenance in the signs and
symbols of Indians without civilized faith.

The traditional ideas of privileged civilizations and their inevitable
expansions over territory held by indigenous populations provide both the
source of and the latent criticism within the American Indian metaphor.
Social Darwinism, which flourished despite the fact that Charles Darwin
himself doubted social and political implications of his theories, reinforces
and legitimizes inequalities of many kinds. Through the artistic perception
of these peculiarly inhuman forms of racism that oppress society comes
the reawakening of "signs and symbols" of human wholeness which the
whole order of American experience betrays.

The metaphorical Indian serves as a victim and as a phantom of the
power-maddened, such as Ahab, but also as a creative and humanizing life

force. This force, as Thoreau observes it, is submerged and haunting; one must dig toward it and the reality the Indian represents:

> The frontiers are not east or west, north or south; but wherever a man fronts a fact, though that fact be his neighbor, there is an unsettled wilderness between him and Canada, between him and the setting sun, or, farther still; between him and it. Let him build himself a log house with the bark on where he is fronting it, and wage there an Old French war for seven or seventy years, with Indians and Rangers, or whatever else may come between him and the reality, and save his scalp if he can.[2]

The ghost of the Indian in the "Old French" Wars of the imagination is not dead; it serves to remind men of what will not die, of that reality" that remains despite a temporary forced exile from the civilized world.

The Indian can be no more an enemy of civilized humanity than civilized humanity appears to be the enemy of itself. Thus, the Indian metaphor is a means of enacting the complexiities and contradictions of civilization and the dangers and threats to it as well, for both the wild and the civilized spring from the same unconscious fears and impulses inherent to man. The rage to power, the intellect that mocks at hope at the same time it desires it, the insoluble nature of conflict without coherence creates a kind of secret despair. The desire to kill the Indian, the "double," the "other," or the rejected part of the self becomes a means of extirpating a threatening image and element of selfhood. It is the genius of the American literary imagination to reimaging a world where the values of hope, equivalence, and amity are restored and reawakened through the figure of the Indian.

The way American literary fictions which contain Indian metaphors end reflects a vision of American experience. The Prairie ends with Leatherstocking's lonely experiment between the worlds of white and

Indian uncompleted only he serves as a mediating force; after his death, the essential conflict. Only temporarily suspended, resumes The imagination of a middle ground between two worlds, which Cooper designs, serves an influential artistic purpose. Thereafter, those who shape Indian metaphor add to and enhance Cooper's fundamentally American creation.

Thoreau orders a creation of the Indian that is a complex of aesthetic and spiritual implication. For Thoreau civilized man tames the natural, wild elements only that he may at last make it more free than he found it. The Indian's wildness at the end of <u>Walden</u> is a means of fronting or confronting men's basic alienation from the natural and wild within in order to achieve a true freedom of imagination and spiritual insight: "Only that day dawns to which we are awake. There is more day to dawn. The sun is but a morning star."[3] If the Indian comes to stand for the dawn of civilization, then those who follow must be reawakened to their origins and their own potential for true selfhood.

For Melville the metaphor of the Indian illuminates the despair of the exploited and the suffering self within. Victims of tyranny in whatever form are absorbed in a single visionary and paradigmatic synthesis at the end of <u>Moby-Dick</u>:

> . . . Gaining that vital center, the black bubble upward burst, and now, liberated by reason of its cunning spring, and owing to its great buoyancy, rising with great force, the Coffin-life buoy shot length wise from the sea, fell over and floated by my side. Buoyed up by that coffin, for almost one whole day and night, I floated on a soft and dirgelike main.[4]

The primal past breaks through from the vortex to sustain the white Ishmael. That very past Ishmael clings to is incomplete; Queequeg's coffin-lifebuoy is empty. Saved temporarily from the terrifying maelstrom, Ishmael struggles on to tell his tale. The conflict of American experience represented by that maelstrom can never be finally resolved, except through the telling of it.

Mark Twain ends The Adventures of Tom Sawyer with lie accidental extermination of Injun Joe. The death of the "bloody-minded outcast" elicits pity and repugnance, but most of all "relief and security."[5] The complex of emotions Tom registers incomplete--horror, partial compassion, vague pleasure--cannot be resolved Tom is simply glad, at least temPorarily, to have done with fear-ridden experience. Injun Joe represents a cosmic giant of horror, who appears like an illness, to threaten and who must be returned to his subterranean cave so that the harmony of St. Petersburg will not be disrupted. Despite Tom's relief at Joe's death, civilization in St Petersburg is not portrayed as suddenly a more humane or established order. Joe's death marks an intermission, only momentary, from the dark and the wild.

The confrontation between atavism and Civilization is reenacted at the end of William Faulkner's Go Down Moses. In this text the conflict is explored internally within the moral and psychological character of a single individual, Ike McCaslin, caught within menacing time and isolating death, Ike's internal conflict cannot be resolved. "No wonder the ruined woods I used to know don't cry for retribution! he thought: the people who have destroyed it will accomplish its revenge."[6] The very form of fiction of Go Down, Moses devolves around a structure that denies linear progression, just as Ike's own experience reflects a development that ends abruptly with the death of the black-Indian, Sam Fathers. Faulkner's vision consists of a range of possibilities based on his perception of man's own nature, not as a given or a stasis, but as a potential, frustrated and oppressed, weak and isolate, yet surviving still, clinging to the shell of knowledge of the primitive past.

Despite the Indian's meaning of despair, horror, and death, white men need to probe it, if only to discover the means to control and define its significance. The distinction of a truly American literature came into being in the formative years of Emerson's generation; it is the same period of the evolution of the Indian metaphor by Cooper, Melville, and Thoreau and that metaphor is derived from and a criticism of the view of American self-interest. As Larzer Ziff observes, the triumph of American "positive nationalism" so necessary for the flourishing of a native literature is based on the full and furious admission that what America wanted most was more land.[7] To dispossess the holders of that land is seen as both deplorable and inevitable. Yet only now the children of the dispossessed, James Welch and N. Scott Momaday, respond with their own truly "native" literature. Their Indian metaphors, like those of the white artists before them, are a preservation of their world. The end of Momaday's House Made of Dawn is emblematic. Abel is active--running endlessly--in getting, in striving. Condemned to a permanent sense of helplessness, he struggles on.

The artists of Indian metaphors represent the complexity and the incompleteness of their view of experience in the context of plot and in the profound, if unsatisfying, idea that the conflicts inherent to white and Indian intermingling in America can never be finally resolved. There is no appearance of finality, except in the structure of the texts themselves. Whether in the incomplete fear of Ishmael, the incomplete pleasure and potential of the narrator of Walden, the incomplete horror of Tom Sawyer, or the incomplete pain of Ike McCaslin, there is always the indeterminate. It is as if the illusion of completeness, like the illusion of civilized order, must be comprehended in order to defend and employ the powers of wildness within all men. From loss, from lack of resolution, the Indian comes to stand as "sign and symbol" for moral resistence and for imaginative affirmation: "hopelessly holding up hope in the midst of despair." The vision within the void defined here is not racial or social; it is universal, an element within experience itself.

NOTES

[1]Herman Melville, <u>Moby-Dick</u>. Ed. Charles Feidelson (New York, 1964), ch. 48, p 301.

[2]Henry David Thoreau, <u>A Week on the Concord and Merrimack Rivers</u>, pp 323-24.

[3]Henry David Thoreau, <u>Walden</u>, p. 333

[4]Herman Melville, <u>Moby-Dick</u>. Ed. by Charles Feidelson. (New York, 1964), epilogue, p. 724.

[5]Mark Twain, <u>The Adventures of Tom Sawyer</u>. (New York,1925),p.267.

[6]William Faulkner, <u>Go Down, Moses</u>. (New York, 1970), p. 364.

[7]Larzer Ziff, <u>Literary Democracy</u>. (New York, 1981), P 300-301.

SELECTED BIBLIOGRAPHY

Included below are works that treat the American Indian at least tangentially or have important implications for its literary history. The bibliography in Paula Gunn Allen's Studies in American Indian Literature (New York, 1983), pp. 320-61; Jeannette Henry, and others' Index to Literature on the American Indian. 4 vols. San Francisco, 1971-1975; and Arlene Hirschfelder's American Indian and Eskimo Authors: A Comprehensive Bibliography (New York, 1973.)

Axtell, James. The Europeans and the Indians: Essays in the Ethnohistory of Colonial North America. New York, 1981.

Barnett, Louise K. The Ignoble Savage: American Literary Racism, 1790-1890. Westport, Conn., 1975.

Berkhofer, Robert F., Jr. The White Man's Indian: Images of the American Indian from Columbus to the Present. New York, 1978.

Bierhorst, John, ed. Four Masterworks of American Indian Literature. New York, 1974.

Chapman, Abraham, ed. Literature of the American Indian: Views and Interpretations. New York, 1975.

Dabney, Lewis. The Indians of Yoknapatawpha. Baton Rouge, La., 1974.

Driver, Harold E. Indians of North America. 2n ed. Chicago, 1969.

Dudley, Edward and Novak, Maximillian, ed. The Wild Man Within. Pittsburgh, 1972.

Elliot, J. H. The Old World and the New, 1492-1650. Cambridge, Eng., 1970.

Fairchild, Hoxie. The Noble Savage. New York, 1961.

Farb, Peter. Man's Rise to Civilization. New York, 1968.

Fiedler, Leslie. The Return of the Vanishing American. New York, 1968.

Fisher, Dexter. The Third Woman: Minority Woman Writers of the United States. New York, 1980.

Foss, Michael. Undreamed Shores. London, 1974.

Fussell, Edwin. Frontier: American Literature and the American West. Princeton, N.J., 1965.

Hallowell, A. Irving. "American Indians, White and Black: The Phenomenon of Transculturalization." Current Anthropology, 4, (1963), 519-31.

Hallowell, A. Irving. "The Backwash of the Frontier: The Impact of the INdian on American Culture." In Walker D. Wyman and Clifton B. Kroeber, eds. The Frontier in Perspective. Madison, Wisc., 1957.

Hanke, Lewis. Aristotle and the American Indian. Bloomington, Ind., 1959.

Harris, Helen. Mark Twain's Response to the Native American," American Literature, XLVI, (January, 1975), 495-505.

Heard, J. Norman. White into Red: A Study of the Assimilation of White Persons Captured by Indians. Metuchen, N.J., 1973.

Hoover, Dwight. The Red and the Black. Chicago, 1976.

Huymes, Dell. "In Vain I Tried to Tell You": Essays in Native American Ethnopoetics. Philadelphia, 1981.

Jacobs, Wilbur R. Dispossessing the American Indian: Indians and Whites on the Colonial Frontier. New York, 1972.

Jennings, Francis. The Invasion of America: Indians, Colonialism, and the Cant of Conquest. Chapel Hill, zn.V., 1975. Part I & II.

Jordan, Winthrop. White Over Black. Chapel Hill, N.C., 1968.

Josephy, Alvin. M. The Indian Heritage of America. New York, 1968.

Keiser, Albert. The Indian in American Literature. New York, 1933.

Keiser, Albert. Thoreau's Manuscripts on the Indian," Journal of English and Germanic Philology XXVIII (April, 1928), 183-199.

Larson, Charles. American Indian Fiction. Albuquerque, 1978.

Levernier, James A., and Hennig Cohen, eds. The Indians and Their Captives. Westport, Conn., 1977.

Lincoln, Kenneth. Native American Renaissance. Berkeley, 1983.

Nash, Gary. Red, White, and Black: The Peoples of Early America. Englewood Cliffs, N.J., 1974.

Pearce, Roy Harvey. The Savages of America: A Study of the Indian and the Idea of Civilization. Baltimore, 1953. Rev. ed. titled Savagism and Civilization: A Study of the Indian and the American Mind. Baltimore, 1965.

Pearce, Roy Harvey. "The Significances of the Captivity Narrative," American Literature, 19 (1947), 1-20.

Philbrick, Francis. The Rise of the West, 1754-1830. New York, 1965.

Porter, H.C. The Inconsistent Savage: England and the North American Indian, 1500-1660. London, 1979.

Rogin, Michael. Fathers and Children. New York, 1975.

Rosowski, Susan, and Helen Stauffer, eds. Women in Western American Literature. Troy, N.Y., 1982.

Rotherberg, Jerome. ed. Shaking and the Pumpkin: Traditional Poetry of the Indian North Americas. Garden City, N.J., 1972.

Sayre, Robert F. "A Bibliography and an Anthology of American Indian Literature," College English, 35 (1974), 704-706.

Sayre, Robert F. Thoreau and the American Indians. Princeton, 1977.

Sheehan, Bernard. W. "Indian-White Relations in Early America: A Review Essay," William and Mary Quarterly, 26 (1969), 267-86.

Sheehan, Bernard.W. Savagism and Civility: Indians and Englishmen in Colonial Virginia. Cambridge, Eng., 1980.

Slotkin, Richard. Regeneration through Violence: The Mythology of the American Frontier, 1600-1860. Middletown, Conn., 1973.

Slotkin, Richard, and James K. Folsom, eds. So Dreadful A Judgment: Puritan Responses to King Philip's War, 1676-1677. Middletown, Conn., 1979.

Stinebeck, David C., and Charles M. Segal. Puritans, Indians, and Manifest Destiny. New York, 1977.

Swann, Brian, ed. Smoothing the Ground: Essays on Native American Oral Literature. Los Angeles, 1982.

Taylor, Golden, ed. The Literary History of the American West. Fort Worth, Texas, 1987.

Trimble, Martha Scott. N. Scott Momaday. Western Writers. Boise, Id., 1973.

124

Turner, Frederick. The Frontier in American History. New York, 1920.

Turner, Victor. The Forest of Symbols. Ithaca, N.Y., 1967.

Underhill, Ruth M. Red Man's America: A History of Indians in the United States. Rev. ed. Chicago, 1971.

VanDerBeets, Richard. Held Captive by Indians: Selected Narratives, 1642-1836. Knoxville, Tenn., 1973.

VanDerBeets, Richard. The Indian Captivity Narrative: An American Genre. Lanham, Md., 1984.

VanDerBeets, Richard. "The Indian Captivity Narrative as Ritual," American Literature, 43 (1972), 548-62.

VanDerBeets, Richard. "A Surfeit of Style: The Indian Captivity Narrative as Penny Dreadful." Research Studies, 39 (1971);, 297-306.

VanDerBeets, Richard. "'A Thirst for Empire': The Indian Captivity Narrative as Propaganda." Research Studies, 40 (1972), 207-215.

Vaughan, Alden T. New England Frontier: Puritans and Indians, 1620-1675. Boston, 1965; rev. ed. New York, 1979.

Vaughan, Alden T. "Pequots and Puritans: The Causes of the War of 1637," William and Mary Quarterly, 21 (1964), 256-69.

Vaughan, Alden T. and Francis J. Bremer, eds. Puritan New England: Essays on Religion Society and Culture. New York, 1977.

Vaughan, Alden T. and Edward C. Clark, eds. Puritans Among the Indians: Accounts of Captivity Redemption. Cambridge, Mass., 1981.

Vaughan, Alden T. and Daniel K. Richter. "Crossing the Cultural Divide: Indians and New Englanders, 1605-1763." American Antiquarian Society Proceedings, 90 (1980), 23-90.

Velie, Alan R. "James Welch's Poetry," American Indian Culture and Research Journal, 3, No. 1 (1979), 19-38.

Velie, Alan R. ed. American Indian Literature: An Anthology. Norman, Okla., 1979.

Velie, Alan R. Four American Indian Literary Masters. Norman, Okla., 1982.

Wallace, Anthony F.C. The Death and Rebirth of the Seneca. New York, 1969.

125

Wallace, Anthony F.C. "Political Organization and Land Tenure Among the Northeastern Indians, 1600-1830." Southwestern Journal of Anthropology. 13 (1957), 301-21.

Washburn, Wilcomb E. The Indian in America. New York, 1975.

Washburn, Wilcomb E. "The Moral and Legal Justification for Dispossessing the Indians." In James Morton Smith ed., Seventeenth-Century America: Essays in Colonial History. Chapel Hill, N.C., 1959.

Washburn, Wilcomb E. Red Man's Land--White Man's Law: A Study of the Past and Present Status of the American Indian. New York, 1971.

Wilner, Eleanor, Gathering the Winds: Visionary Imagination and Radical Transformation of Self and Society. Baltimore, Md., 1975.

Ziff, Larzer. Literary Democracy: The Declaration of Cultural Independence in America. New York, 1981.

Ziff, Larzer. Puritanism in America: New Culture in a New World. New York, 1973.

Zolla, Elemire. The Writer and the Shaman. Trans. Raymond Rosenthal. New York, 1973.

INDEX

128

STUDIES IN AMERICAN LITERATURE